the ULTIMATE *Days of Our Lives*
TRIVIA BOOK

the ULTIMATE
Days of Our Lives
TRIVIA BOOK

GERARD J. WAGGETT

RENAISSANCE BOOKS
Los Angeles

Copyright © 1999 by Gerard J. Waggett

All rights reserved. Reproduction without permission in writing from the publisher is prohibited, except for brief passages in connection with a review. For permission, write: Renaissance Books, 5858 Wilshire Boulevard, Suite 200, Los Angeles, California 90036.

Photo Credits:
 © Albert Ortega/Flower Children, Ltd.—pages 14, 19, 25, 31, 35, 41, 52, 59, 62, 69, 79, 82, 93, 101, 108, 114, 116, 119, 121, 125, 147, 149, 154, 164, 176, 179

© Sue Schneider/Flower Children, Ltd.—pages 46, 89 (right), 127 (both), 133

© Paul Fenton/Flower Children, Ltd.—page 89 (left)

Cover Photo Credits:
Jenson Ackles photograph © Paul Fenton/Flower Children, Ltd.; all other photographs © Albert Ortega/Flower Children, Ltd.

Library of Congress Cataloging-in-Publication Data

Waggett, Gerard J.

    The ultimate Days of our lives trivia book / Gerard J. Waggett.

        p. cm.

    Includes bibliographical references and index.

    ISBN 1-58063-049-9 (trade paper : alk. paper)

    1. Days of our lives (Television program)—Miscellanea.

    I. Title.

    PN1992.77.D38W35   1999

    791.45'72—dc21   98-51395

                                                CIP

10 9 8 7 6 5 4 3 2 1

Design by Susan Shankin

Manufactured in the United States

Distributed by St. Martin's Press

First Edition

For my agents,
Frank Coffey and Frank Weimann,
who have made all this happen

Contents

QUIZZES

Acknowledgments

I AM GRATEFUL TO MY EDITOR, Brenda Scott Royce, for taking on this project even though she's been a longtime fan of *As the World Turns*. As I hope she's learned from working on this book with me, the two shows' histories are more closely linked than viewers checking them out nowadays would guess.

As my dedication states, my agents, Frank Coffey and Frank Weimann, have made yet another book deal happen for me.

I also owe thanks to my family, which continues to be a source of support for my career: my mother Barbara Waggett, my father Fred Waggett, my brothers Freddy, Michael, and Kevin; my sisters-in-law Keri, Christine, and Julie; my nieces Taylor, Norma, and Ava; my nephew Matthew; my aunt Margaret Connolly; my uncles Eddie and Jackie Connolly; and my cousin Mabel Waggett.

I also need to single out some friends who have been a great help to me in putting this book together whether they realize it or not: my roommate Jamie Walsh, R. Scott Reedy, Don Casali, and Rae Costello.

Thanks also to Sue Schneider of Flower Children, Ltd. for providing a great selection of photos.

Lastly, two people in particular helped me gather information for this book. Lauren Hanover remains a great fountain of knowledge about the soap industry. I only wish half the secrets she knows were suitable for print. Beth Porchey gave permission to use information from her Web site, Beth's *Days of Our Lives* Page (**http://www.stl-online.net/days/**), easily the most comprehensive Web site devoted to *Days* that I came across in my Net surfing. Anyone still hungry for information about *Days* after they finish reading this book should definitely check it out.

Introduction

DURING THE LATE 1970s to mid-'80s, my TV set stayed on ABC all afternoon, from 12:30 until 4:00 P.M. I wasn't interested in checking out other soaps—no matter how much other students in my dorm raved about *Days of Our Lives*. When I realized that I wanted to make some career for myself connected to the soaps, possibly writing about them, I decided to broaden my horizons and check out what NBC and CBS had to offer. *Days of Our Lives* provided the same combination of spy games and crime drama that had originally pulled me into *General Hospital*. Collected below are my favorite storylines and moments from the thirteen years and counting that I've been following the lives of the Hortons, Bradys, DiMeras, and other residents of Salem.

the SHANE/KIMBERLY/VICTOR/CAROLINE/ SHAWN PENTANGLE (1985)

Estranged from Shane and blind, Kimberly Brady took up with Salem's latest millionaire crime boss, Victor Kiriakis, who still carried a torch for her mother Caroline. The complicated relationship blended together beautifully with the ongoing crime drama as Kimberly slept with Victor to distract him from his plan to kill Shane.

BO LEARNS HE'S VICTOR'S SON (1986)

Bo Brady held a gun on family enemy Victor Kiriakis. To keep Bo from pulling the trigger, Caroline Brady blurted out that Victor was his father. It was one of those cliffhangers that had me counting the sands through the hourglass until the next episode.

All about Eve (1987)

Long before Sami Brady ever tried to sell her baby sister on the black market, Eve Donovan was Salem's resident Bad Seed. She made life hell for her stepmother Kimberly, ultimately bringing about her miscarriage. Eve also sold her body on the street and fell in love with her pimp. Charlotte Ross more than earned her two Emmy nominations as the most fascinatingly complex teen character to set foot in Salem.

the Riverfront Knifer (1988)

I might not have enjoyed this serial killer storyline as much if I had been watching while the Salem Strangler and Salem Slasher slayed their way through town, but it was a fascinating double-edged mystery: guessing who the killer was as well as who the next victim would be.

Vivian Buries Carly Alive/The Lobotomy (1993-94)

Taking a page from Edgar Allan Poe, Vivian Alamain buried Carly Manning alive. Louise Sorel played out Vivian's demented side, rolling around on top of Carly's grave. Months later, Vivian was strapped to an operating table and shaved bald, as a corrupt doctor prepared to lobotomize her. It was a visually striking scene as well as a great counterpoint to burying Carly alive.

Sami Shoots Alan Harris in the Groin (1995)

From Bill Horton to Jack Deveraux to Lawrence Alamain, too many rapists on the show had been transformed into romantic leads. Though painful for me as a man to watch, it was also gratifying to see one rapist get what he had coming to him.

The Years of Our Lives

EARLY 1960S: Irna Phillips, who created such power-house soaps as *The Guiding Light* and *As the World Turns*, along with her *ATWT* director Ted Corday and Allan Chase came up with the idea for *Days of Our Lives* while sitting on the front porch of a house in Southampton, New York. Not surprisingly, at the outset *Days* bore a strong resemblance to *As the World Turns*, the show Phillips and Corday had been working on together since 1956. Like the Hughes family on *ATWT*, the Hortons were an upper middle class family living in a small Midwestern town. While Chris and Nancy Hughes were raising a family of four, Tom and Alice Horton had three grown children living at home and one granddaughter, Julie, a troubled teen just like Penny Hughes, who had proven to be a popular character with the *ATWT* audience.

July 13–14, 1965: The pilot for *Days of Our Lives* was filmed at the NBC Burbank studios, directed by Joe Behar, who had also directed the pilot for *General Hospital*. For the pilot, the epigraph read: "Each day is a little life, every waking and rising, a little breath. Every fresh morning, a little youth. Every rest and sleep a little death; and the sands are running through the hourglass."

September 27, 1965: *Morning Star* and *Paradise Bay*, two soaps created by Ted Corday, debuted in morning time slots on NBC.

November 1, 1965: The first episode was taped. The first week of shows needed to be re-taped because the lighting was completely off.

The legendary Macdonald Carey (Dr. Tom Horton)

November 8, 1965: The first episode of *Days of Our Lives* was broadcast on NBC at 2:00 in the afternoon. The episode received a lukewarm review in *Variety*, which complimented its "many warm and winning moments," but also deemed the show "unsophisticated." This first episode has subsequently been made available to the public for viewing at the Museum of Television and Radio in New York City.

1966: Days of Our Lives was ranked thirty-second out of thirty-four shows on daytime. *Morning Star* and *Paradise Bay* were both canceled later that year on the same day, July 1. NBC gave *Days* thirteen weeks to pull up its ratings or join Corday's other two soaps in oblivion. Bill Bell, who was penning the top-rated soap *As the World Turns,* took a leave of absence to do what he could with *Days.* At first, Bell planned to write both shows, but he soon realized that he needed to focus all his energy on *Days.* Although eager to take on the challenge of making *Days* work, Bell was nervous. He has often commented that he lost ten pounds during his first week on the job. Bell, who had dealt with gang rape on *As the World Turns* and abortion on *Another World,* brought his gift for topical, controversial storytelling to *Days* with tales of incest and water pollution.

1966: Ted Corday died. His wife, Betty, took his place as executive producer. Among her first moves was to bring on board as a producer H. Wesley Kenney, who had been directing *The Doctors,* which followed *Days* on NBC.

1967: One of Bill Bell's most powerful stories involved the death of infant Richard Martin. Not long after Richard was born, his father, David, accidentally killed him while playing with him on a swing. Richard's grief-stricken mother, Susan, shot and killed David. As young Richard lay in the hospital dying, fans wrote in to the show, begging Bill Bell not to let the child die. Bell was moved by the letters but had not gotten to read them until after the scenes in which Richard died had already been taped. Although the trial in which Susan was acquitted of killing David by reason of temporary insanity boosted the show's ratings, Bell swore that he would never again kill a baby on his shows. Some twenty-odd years later, however, he did kill off an infant on *The Young and the Restless.*

1968: A drunken Bill Horton raped his ex-girlfriend Laura Spencer Horton, who was then married to his brother Mickey. Laura subsequently became pregnant. The paternity of her son, Mike, would become one of daytime's longest kept secrets. Laura would eventually work her way back to Bill, setting a dangerous precedent for rape-triggered romances on daytime. The most famous rape-triggered romance in daytime history—that of Luke Spencer and Laura Webber on *General Hospital*—was written by Pat Falken Smith, who had worked with Bill Bell on the Bill/Laura/Mickey triangle. Ironically, when *General Hospital's* Laura Webber finally married Luke Spencer, her name became Laura Spencer.

1969: The triangle involving Laura Horton, her husband Mickey, and his brother Bill proved so popular and such an audience draw that other soap operas began to copy the idea. Even longtime veterans such as *As the World Turns* and *The Guiding Light,* whose ratings had dropped a few notches in the late 1960s, introduced storylines in which two brothers fell in love with the same woman. On *Guiding Light,* one brother was a lawyer, the other a doctor—just like Bill and Mickey Horton. In the *As the World Turns* triangle, Elizabeth Talbot became pregnant by Dan Stewart but married his brother, Paul.

1970: Singer Bill Hayes joined the cast as con artist/lounge singer Brent Douglas/Doug Williams. Doug's romance with Julie Olson, coupled with Hayes's real-life romance with Susan Seaforth, the actress who played Julie, turned the pair into the show's first supercouple.

November 1971: *Days of Our Lives* knocked *As the World Turns* out of the top spot in the Nielsen ratings for a week. Making this coup somewhat ironic, Bill Bell had left his head-writing duties on *As the World Turns* to help pull up *Days'* ratings.

1972: Addie Olson Williams bought Sergio's nightclub for her new husband Doug Williams. Renamed Doug's Place, the site served as a venue for singer-actors Bill Hayes (DOUG) and Robert Clary (ROBERT LECLAIR) to perform. Although other soaps had previously incorporated popular music into their storylines, the setting of Doug's Place has often been credited with popularizing the use of contemporary music on daytime television.

1973: General Hospital lured away actress Denise Alexander, who had played the tragic heroine Susan Hunter since 1966, with what was at the time estimated to be the largest salary paid to a daytime performer.

1974: Producer-director Wes Kenney left the show to direct the top-rated sitcom *All in the Family.*

1975: After nine years, Susan Flannery left the role of Dr. Laura Horton. The producers' disappointment in her replacements—Susan Oliver and then Rosemary Forsyth—would lead them to create a brand new female psychiatrist, Dr. Marlena Evans—the role that would make Deidre Hall famous.

April 21, 1975: Days expanded to an hour, the second soap opera to do so. Wes Kenney was lured back to helm the show. The expansion to an hourlong show created extremely long workdays, often running from seven in the morning until midnight. Among the changes Kenney instituted to better accommodate the hourlong format: The show no longer taped in the sequence in which it aired; instead, entire sequences that took place in one setting would be filmed start to finish and edited later on. NBC pushed the show's starting time back to 1:30, putting it head-to-head against *As the World Turns.* Although *Days* had occasionally toppled *ATWT* from its number one spot, overall *As the World Turns* remained the more popular soap opera. Some critics have pointed to this scheduling change as one of the reasons *Days'* ratings began to slide in the mid-1970s.

January 12, 1976: A scene still from *Days of Our Lives* featuring Bill Hayes and Susan Seaforth Hayes was pictured on the cover of *Time* magazine. Titled "Sex and Suffering in the Afternoon," the cover story explored the world of soap operas and named *Days* and Bill Bell's other show, *The Young and the Restless,* as the best soaps on the air. The article described *Days* as "the most daring drama, encompassing every trend from artificial insemination to interracial romance."

September 16, 1976: The first union between Doug Williams and Julie Olson was treated like a royal wedding, which, to daytime audiences, it was. Doug and Julie were the show's premier couple, and their portrayers, married in real life, had become the First Couple of Daytime Television. On the day Doug and Julie finally married *each other*, some four thousand fans turned out at the NBC studios in Burbank, where the show was taped, to watch the wedding on monitors that had been specially set up for the occasion. At the end of the show, Bill Hayes and Susan Seaforth Hayes, dressed in their characters' wedding finery, stepped outside to greet their "wedding guests." Some took pictures; others threw rice.

1976—77: Hate mail poured in to the show after Valerie Grant, a black woman, kissed David Banning, a white man. So great and so negative was the response that the show decided to jettison the interracial romance storyline. Pat Falken Smith, head writer at the time, believes that the audience might have accepted David and Valerie as a couple if the show had married them off before showing them kiss.

1976—77: Days broke ground on daytime once again with two storylines touching upon the previously taboo subject of homosexuality. When Mike Horton (then played by Wesley Eure) didn't feel comfortable making love to his girlfriend Trish Clayton, he worried that he might be a homosexual. He talked about his worries with Linda Anderson, who slept with Mike to prove that he wasn't gay. A year later, Julie Williams was redecorating the home of a couple, Karl and Sharon Duval, when she realized that both the husband *and* the wife were interested in her sexually. Julie turned them both down, and the Duvals were written off the show shortly thereafter.

1977: When asked if there was any actor or actress with whom she would like to work, Deidre Hall replied her identical twin sister Andrea. Shortly thereafter, Andrea Hall-Lovell joined the show as Marlena's identical twin sister, Samantha. It was the first time on daytime that identical twins played identical twins.

1977—78: Pat Falken Smith left her position as head writer because of a contract dispute. In the years until she returned in 1981, the show went through five different head writers/head-writing teams. With each turnover, the ratings sank further and further.

1979: Despite the declining ratings, NBC considered expanding *Days* from an hour to ninety minutes as it had done with *Another World.*

In 1980, Marlena Evans (Deidre Hall) was nearly written off the show.

No other soap opera heroine has gone through the same sort of ordeals as Dr. Marlena Evans. She's been kidnapped more times than either she or the audience would care to remember. She's had more than her share of guns pointed at her and has slipped into more than one coma. Of course, all of that put together pales in comparison to being possessed by Satan himself.

1. What was the name of Marlena's twin sister who took over Marlena's life and stuck her in a sanitarium?

(a) Justine   (b) Janet   (c) Maggie   (d) Samantha

2. Which of Salem's varied serial killers frequently called into Marlena's radio show?

(a) The Salem Strangler   (b) The Salem Slasher

(c) The Riverfront Knifer   (d) The Sin Stalker

3. Who planned to kill Marlena on live television while disguised as Roman Brady?

(a) André DiMera   (b) Stefano DiMera

(c) Kellam Chandler   (d) Alex Marshall

4. For whose murder did Marlena go on trial in 1985?

(a) Roman Brady   (b) Emma Donovan

(c) Nick Corelli   (d) Stefano DiMera

5. How was Marlena presumed killed in the late 1980s?

(a) in a car crash   (b) in a plane crash

(c) in a cave-in   (d) in a lab explosion

6. Why did Marlena's daughter Sami try to sell her baby sister Belle on the black market?

(a) to support her drug habit

(b) because she knew that John Black and not her father Roman was Belle's real father

(c) to punish her parents for breaking up her romance with Austin Reed

(d) because she had been brainwashed by Stefano DiMera

7. Who imprisoned Marlena in the boiler pit of an abandoned warehouse?

(a) Stella Lombard   (b) Vivian Alamain

(c) Stefano Dimera   (d) Alex Marshall

8. What was the name of the New Orleans mansion where Stefano held Marlena and John hostage?

(a) Journey's End   (b) Maison Blanche

(c) Maison Noir   (d) Wildwind

9. In what foreign capital did Stefano keep Marlena locked up in a golden cage?

(a) London   (b) Paris   (c) Rome   (d) Moscow

10. In what part of John Black's house did Kristen Blake imprison Marlena for weeks on end during the summer of 1997?

(a) the attic   (b) the wine cellar

(c) the pantry   (d) the pool house

1980: Dubbed the Valentine's Day Massacre, a total of fourteen characters were written off by head writer Nina Laemmle within a six-month period. Among the actors left unemployed: Mark Tapscott (BOB ANDERSON), Eileen Barnett (BROOKE HAMILTON), Suzanne Zenor (MARGO HORTON), Margaret Mason (LINDA ANDERSON), Robert Clary (ROBERT LECLAIR),

Rosemary Forsyth (DR. LAURA HORTON), and Edward Mallory (BILL HORTON). During this same six-month period, nine new characters were introduced, few of whom survived more than a year or two. The most popular character brought on during this period was singer Liz Curtis, played by Gloria Loring. Because of the large number of departures, the practice of commemorating a performer's final day with cake and champagne was done away with. And as hard as it is to imagine *Days* without Deidre Hall, Marlena Evans was one of the characters that was seriously considered to be written off.

1981: The Salem Strangler storyline began as Dr. Marlena Evans received phone calls during her radio show from a serial killer who preyed upon women he deemed immoral. The storyline marked a new direction for the show, turning its focus away from psychological drama and onto crime drama. During the 1980s alone, two more serial killers (the Salem Slasher and the Riverfront Knifer) would stalk the show, as well as a serial rapist.

1982: The writers pulled off one of the show's most controversial Friday cliffhangers when the Salem Strangler presumably killed Marlena Evans. The switchboards at NBC lit up with complaints while fans arrived outside the NBC studios to form a picket line. In an effort to appease the crowd, Deidre Hall herself came out to assure the picketers that Marlena was not dead and that all would be revealed on Monday. The incident made national news, boosting the ratings for the following Monday (a holiday at that), when the audience learned that it was actually Marlena's twin sister, Samantha, who had been murdered by the Strangler.

April 7, 1982: Brenda Benet, who played the villainous Lee Dumonde, took her own life with a handgun. The suicide took place one year after the death of her six-year-old son, Christopher. Due to the tragic circumstances, the show decided not to recast the role even though the character had yet to reveal that her daughter Renée's father was Stefano DiMera. Scripts were rewritten so that the secret was revealed in a letter Lee had written before leaving town. Philece Sampler, who played Renée, considered the scene in which she read the letter the most difficult she had ever played. A memorial service for Benet was held in the home of her castmate Lanna Sanders (MARIE HORTON).

1983: Days of Our Lives moved production from Stage 9 on the NBC Burbank lot to a studio in Hollywood. Frances Reid (ALICE HORTON) made it to the new studio the first day without incident, but the following day went by force of habit back to Burbank.

1983: The wedding of Dr. Marlena Evans and police officer Roman Brady was the show's most anticipated union since Doug married Julie back in 1976. The wedding, which aired over four days, was filled with the sort of adventure (in the form of an assassination attempt) and romance that had made Marlena and Roman the show's most popular couple. Deidre Hall and Wayne Northrop celebrated the wedding with not one but two offscreen receptions. NBC hosted a party at Chasen's restaurant in Los Angeles for members of the press and industry hot-shots; later Hall and Northrop headed to the Sportsmen's Lodge in the San Fernando Valley for a second reception with their fans.

1984: Doug and Julie Williams, who had dominated Days of Our Lives during the 1970s, were written off into the sunset. Bill Hayes and Susan Seaforth Hayes had turned down the show's offer to remain at a reduced salary and with no promise of any storyline. Word on the set during this time was that there would be no more stories written for characters over thirty-five years old. One of the factors that bothered Seaforth Hayes about Doug and Julie's departure was that the show did not send them off in any blaze of glory. Their last scene showed the two of them packing for a long trip. Bill and Susan Seaforth Hayes returned for separate stints later in the 1980s, then in 1993 their characters were reunited and written off once again. They have since returned to the show for a number of guest spots.

1985: While Bill and Susan Seaforth Hayes may have wished for a better swan song, at the very least, their last scene had some sense of finality to it.

Jed Allan (DON CRAIG) had by the mid-1980s been with *Days* for fourteen years, most of those as a leading man. As such, he probably expected some sort of official send off. But Don Craig didn't even get one of those out-of-town jobs. No, in a scene that has become legendary in daytime for its sense of anti-climax, Don Craig went out to mail a letter and was never heard from again.

1986: "Friends and Lovers," which was used as a love theme for Shane and Kimberly and was sung by Gloria Loring (LIZ CURTIS) and Carl Anderson, hit number two on *Billboard*'s Hot 100, making it one of the most popular songs of the year and one of few songs popularized directly because of its association with a soap opera. The following year, "At This Moment," another Shane and Kimberly theme, would top the *Billboard* charts, helped along not only by its exposure on *Days,* but also from its use on the widely popular Michael J. Fox sitcom *Family Ties.*

1987: Genie Francis, who had made daytime history as half of *General Hospital*'s supercouple Luke and Laura, joined the show as newspaper reporter Diana Colville around the same time that Dr. Marlena Evans was being killed off. Some fans took umbrage at Francis's hiring, believing it to be nothing more than a public relations move designed to offset the loss of Hall. The higher-ups at *Days* heard that these outraged fans were planning a picket line to rival the one formed five years earlier when Marlena had been presumably killed. Deidre Hall herself was rumored to have been contacted about putting an end to the picket line before it started.

1988: The writers union went on strike. While the show continued to be produced and written, the writers' strike did take its toll in a number of ways. One plan to introduce a gay character or have an existing character come out of the closet was scratched. The interim writers also took a brainwashing storyline head writer Leah Laiman had intended for Shane Donovan and rewrote it for John Black.

July 25, 1988: Although Bo and Hope are considered *Days'* premier couple of the 1980s, it was the wedding of Steve "Patch" Johnson and Kayla Brady that gave the show its all-time highest ratings.

1989: Production of *Days of Our Lives* moved from the Hollywood studio back to Burbank, but not to the original soundstage. That had been taken over by another NBC soap opera, *Santa Barbara*. On the first day at the new studio, both John Aniston (VICTOR KIRIAKIS) and James Reynolds (ABE CARVER) got lost and wound up in the middle of an NBC studio tour. When they tried to break away from the tour to get into the *Days* studios, a guard who didn't recognize the actors tried to stop them.

1989: Despite protests from Stephen Nichols, the show de-patched Patch. In the storyline, Steve Johnson underwent high-tech surgery and was implanted with a false eye so that he could infiltrate the camp of a white supremist organization. Fans didn't take to a patchless Patch, so several months down the line, the new eye was smashed during a fight and the eye patch was back where it belonged.

Stephen Nichols wearing Steve Johnson's namesake eye patch.

1989: In a move that reminded many of the Valentine's Day Massacre of 1980, eleven actors were taken off contract or let go altogether. Among them: Suzanne Rogers (MAGGIE HORTON), John Clarke (MICKEY HORTON), Peggy McCay (CAROLINE BRADY), Frank Parker (SHAWN BRADY), and James Reynolds (ABE CARVER). Within a year or two, several of the actors were put back on contract.

1990: Peter Reckell and Kristian Alfonso returned to the show after a period of three years away. While Alfonso stayed only for a couple of months, just long enough for Hope to be presumably killed off, Reckell stayed on. He was the first of many popular performers from the 1980s whom the show managed to lure back in the '90s.

1990: After scoring its all-time highest ratings in 1988, *Days* lost more than a million viewers in the following two years and slipped down to number eight in the ratings.

1991: *Days of Our Lives* lured back not only Deidre Hall but also Wayne Northrop, who had played Roman to her Marlena in the early 1980s. Northrop's return presented the show with a particularly tricky predicament. Drake Hogestyn, who had replaced Northrop as Roman via the plastic surgery convention, had proven himself extremely popular with the fans, too popular to simply dump. The writers, therefore, came up with a storyline in which Hogestyn's Roman turned out to be a plant whom arch-criminal Stefano DiMera had brainwashed into thinking he was Roman Brady. That twist has sent Hogestyn's Roman—John Black as he now calls himself—on a long (as in still unfinished) search for his true identity. When Hogestyn first joined the show, it should be noted, the writers themselves were not sure if he would turn out to be Roman or not. Visually, the storyline made little sense. Even accepting the premise that John Black had undergone extensive plastic surgery on his face, the men were different body types and heights. Despite all the plotline somersaults the writers had done to have both Hogestyn and Northrop on the show, Northrop was written off only a couple of years after his return.

January 10, 1992: *Days of Our Lives* aired its first episode in primetime (8:00 P.M.). Billed as a mini-movie event, "One Stormy Night" preceded the first primetime airing of the *Soap Opera Digest* awards. The episode picked up where that day's installment had left off and was set against the backdrop of a rainstorm. Because of the evening time slot, the episode was broadcast in a film-look video. "One Stormy Night" earned a 10.5 rating.

1992: For the first time in twenty-seven years, *Days of Our Lives* updated its opening, changing from a still picture of an hourglass to an animated version where viewers could see the sands actually running through the hourglass.

1992: *Days of Our Lives* introduced the mall Salem Place, daytime's first permanent outdoor set. The set was constructed in the section of the NBC parking lot where crowds once gathered prior to the studio tour.

1992: The show really wanted to keep the resolution to the *Who Killed Nick Corelli?* mystery as much of a mystery as possible. Nine different characters were taped pulling the trigger. As it turned out, the until-then virtuous Jo Johnson was revealed to be the killer, blaming Nick for the death of her son Steve.

February 26, 1993: For its second primetime episode, "Night Sins," *Days* abandoned the film look. Once again, the special preceded that year's *Soap Opera Digest* awards ceremony. "Night Sins" was set mainly against the backdrop of the black tie gala Victor Kiriakis (John Aniston) was throwing to launch his new publishing empire. The episode pulled in an 8.0 in the ratings, down 2.5 points from the previous year.

1993: With *Days of Our Lives* ranked number eight out of ten soaps, NBC conducted a study to determine whether or not the show would benefit from a different time slot. *Days'* competitors for the 1:00–2:00 timeslot—*The Young and the Restless* and *The Bold and the Beautiful* on CBS and *All My Children* on ABC—were then the three highest-rated soaps on daytime.

February 1994: Television coverage of the earthquake that devastated Los Angeles pre-empted *Days of Our Lives*. While pre-emptions don't normally pose much of a problem—the schedule just gets pushed back a day—the earthquake delays created problems for the special primetime episode "Winter Dreams." The producers agreed that the episode of *Days* that would air on Friday needed to be re-edited so that it moved smoothly into that evening's primetime special. So, amidst aftershocks from the quake, executive producer Tom Langan and head writer James Reilly sat in Reilly's backyard plotting out the necessary adjustments. "Winter Dreams," most memorable for its image of Vivian Alamain (Louise Sorel) strapped down to an operating table and shaved bald for a midnight lobotomy, pulled in a rating of 8.1. Although it scored a higher rating than 1993's "Night Sins," there has yet to be a fourth episode specially produced for primetime.

March 21, 1994: Macdonald Carey died from cancer less than a week after his eighty-first birthday. Three months later, his character Tom Horton died on the show. Among the former *Days* stars who returned for the onscreen funeral were Maree Cheatham (the original MARIE HORTON), Bill and Susan Seaforth Hayes (DOUG and JULIE WILLIAMS), and Lisa Trusel (MELISSA HORTON). Executive producer Ken Corday, who had known Carey for practically his (Corday's) entire life, could not bear to watch the funeral. As a lasting tribute to his memory, Carey's voice is still heard during the epigraph: "Like sands through the hourglass so are the days of our lives." The rest of the opening, in which viewers used to hear him say, "I'm Macdonald Carey . . . " has been cut.

July 8, 1994: The O. J. Simpson murder investigation wreaked havoc with soap opera schedules from 1993 until 1994. To help accommodate for the pre-emptions, NBC broadcast two episodes of *Days* in primetime, running them from 9:00 to 11:00 P.M.

1994—95: After toying around at the edge of the supernatural with Stefano DiMera's numerous resurrections and his cohort Celeste's psychic abilities, James Reilly pulled out all the stops when lead heroine Marlena

Evans was possessed by Satan. After months of bedeviling Salem (burning down Christmas trees, desecrating churches, sending swarms of bees after her ex-father-in-law), Marlena was exorcised by her amnesiac ex-lover John Black, who had recently discovered that he used to be a priest. The storyline drew a lot of criticism from members of the press as well as the audience. Some complained that the storyline crossed the line in terms of believable material soap operas should be dealing with; others objected from a moral point of view, especially disturbed that the show had begun the storyline right before Christmas, one of the holiest times of the year. Some NBC affiliates actually ran messages along the bottom of the screen during the show stating that the contents of the program did not reflect the views of the station.

1995: Despite all the protests, the Satanic possession storyline helped *Days* pull in more than half a million new fans—enough to propel the show from number six in the soap opera ratings to number two. Making the audience boost even more impressive, *Days* increased its viewership when every other soap—save the top-rated *Young and the Restless*—was losing fans. Other soaps followed *Days'* lead: *All My Children* introduced a voodoo plotline, *Guiding Light* brought an angel into town, and *Another World* toyed with a vampire storyline.

1995: In a story so big that it merited back-to-back covers of *Soap Opera Digest*, Peter Reckell returned to the show as Bo Brady, replacing his own replacement, Robert Kelker-Kelly, who had proven himself a worthy successor both in talent and popularity, evidenced by a pair of *Soap Opera Digest* awards. According to press releases from the show, Reckell was brought back so that the show could make use of old clips of him and Kristian Alfonso as Bo and Hope. Talk behind the scenes had it that Kelker-Kelly was hard to work with. *TV Guide's* Michael Logan wrote in one column that Alfonso made the show choose between him and her.

December 10, 1995: ABC aired the made-for-television movie *Never Say Never: The Deidre Hall Story*, chronicling the actress's infertility and the birth of her son through a surrogate mother. The TV movie was originally planned for NBC, but Hall and the peacock network didn't share the same vision for the project. In the film, Hall played herself as did Wayne Northrop, Northrop's wife Lynn Herring, Hall's twin sister Andrea, Suzanne Rogers, and John de Lancie. NBC, it should be noted, at one point optioned the TV-movie rights to Patsy Pease's life story chronicling her abusive childhood, but never produced the film.

1996: Days did a crossover of sorts with the hit NBC sitcom *Friends.* In the course of an ongoing storyline, Joey Tribiani (Matt LeBlanc's character) was cast on *Days* as Dr. Drake Ramoré. The name, some have speculated, was a parody on Drake Hogestyn, whose trademark eyebrow arch LeBlanc seemed to spoof in a number of scenes. Roark Critchlow (DR. MIKE HORTON) occasionally popped up alongside LeBlanc in hospital scenes. Joey's tenure on the show came to an end after he made some ill-advised remarks to *Soap Opera Digest.* Head writer James Reilly made a brief cameo, seen only from the back, in the episode where Dr. Drake Ramoré is killed after falling down an elevator shaft. The story arc took great license with geography: *Days* is taped in Los Angeles while *Friends* is set in New York City.

March 21, 1997: Days taped its 8,000th episode.

1997: NBC, wanting to build up the number of soaps it owns, lured away *Days'* head writer James E. Reilly with the offer to create his own soap opera. Even after stepping down as head writer, Reilly remained on *Days* in the capacity of consultant and took on consulting duties at NBC's fledgling soap *Sunset Beach* as well.

December 24, 1997: In the Christmas Eve episode, Eileen Davidson and the technical crew pull off a daytime first when all four characters Davidson had been playing on the show (KRISTEN BLAKE, SUSAN BANKS, SISTER MARY MOIRA BANKS, and THOMAS BANKS) appeared in the same scene together.

1998: Columbia TriStar, which distributes *Days,* ticked off NBC and its affiliates by signing a deal with the satellite service DirecTV, allowing each day's episode to be rebroadcast several times without commercials the same night. Columbia used a loophole in its contract with NBC that did not forbid selling rebroadcasting rights. Columbia claimed that it was trying to help build and maintain the show's audience by allowing viewers a second and third chance to catch an episode they may have missed during the day. It has been estimated that as many as fifty thousand viewers, or roughly 1 percent of the show's audience, shelled out $1.49 per day to watch *Days* on DirecTV. More than a few NBC affiliates, who believe that exclusivity should be part of the deal, called for the network to dump the show.

Despite Robert Kelker-Kelly's popularity as Bo Brady, he was replaced by his predecessor, Peter Reckell.

Casting Stories

WHEN TED CORDAY was starting up *Days of Our Lives*, he wanted a name actor in the role of Tom Horton, someone whose mere presence on the show would drum up interest. Although it was considered quite a step down in an actor's career to go from starring in films to working on daytime television, Macdonald Carey accepted Corday's offer because he was desperate for work. Between 1942 and 1962, Carey had made roughly thirty films and appeared in a number of plays, two of them on Broadway (*Anniversary Waltz* and *Lady in the Dark*). Since 1962, though, stage, film, and even primetime roles were coming fewer and further between. Accepting the role of Dr. Tom Horton brought Carey's career full circle—back in the late 1930s, he played a doctor on the radio soap *Woman in White*, which, like *Days*, was created by Irna Phillips.

Although Frances Reid has played Alice Horton for the past thirty-three years, she was not the original choice for the role. Mary Jackson, who would go on to play one of the Baldwin sisters on *The Waltons*, filmed the original pilot for *Days of Our Lives*. The producers didn't think that Jackson had enough chemistry with Macdonald Carey, so Reid was called in to replace her. When Ted Corday offered her the role, he asked, "Do you want to do a job for ten years?" Reid, who had been acting for many years by this point, laughed and answered, "Nothing lasts for ten years." She has now been with the show for more than three decades.

The first time Susan Seaforth Hayes read for the role of Julie Olson, the show passed her over because her eyelashes were too long.

When *Days of Our Lives* was first being cast, Frank Parker read for the role of Bill Horton. Although Ted and Betty Corday were impressed with his performance, they felt that he was too young for the role. Ever the gracious loser, Parker suggested that they check out a friend of his by the name of Edward Mallory. As it turned out, the Cordays were familiar with Mallory and were already considering him for the part. Parker, who would do a couple of smaller roles (once as a car salesman, another as a doctor) would finally join the cast almost two decades later as Shawn Brady.

Edward Mallory, meanwhile, had been hired to play leading man Bill Riley on Ted Corday's other soap opera, *Morning Star*. After NBC decided to drop *Morning Star*, Corday offered Mallory the role of Bill Horton, which was being recast. As it turned out, the last week of *Morning Star* overlapped with Mallory's first week as Bill. While the overlap made for twice as much memorization for Mallory, the logistics worked out beautifully for him. The two shows were taped at different times in the same studio. So, for his first week as Bill Horton, Mallory spent half the day taping *Morning Star* and the other half taping *Days of Our Lives* down the hall.

Long before he ever started playing Victor Kiriakis, John Aniston auditioned for the role of Doug Williams. For his screen test, the producers asked him to shave off his mustache. He complied, not that it helped him land the role. Bill Hayes was hired to play Doug, but the producers decided that Aniston would be perfect for the role of Eric Richards, the doctor at the prison where Doug and Bill Horton were incarcerated. The producers just had one stipulation for Aniston: They wanted him to grow back his mustache.

Joan Van Ark originally took the role of model Janene Whitney mainly because she had recently given birth and wanted to test herself to see if she could still memorize dialogue.

Macdonald Carey was none too pleased when Patricia Barry was hired to play his daughter Addie. He considered himself too young to have a daughter Barry's age. He and Barry had, in fact, previously played lovers on a couple of TV series. Eventually, he accepted the casting and worked quite well with Barry.

Mary Frann was originally called in to see if she would be interested in taking over the role of Susan Hunter after Denise Alexander departed for *General Hospital*. Not only was Frann not interested in taking over a role that had been originated by another actress, she was especially not interested in one that had been played by someone as immensely popular as Alexander had been. She declined the offer and took a role on the short-lived soap *Return to Peyton Place*, where she was paired with Joe Gallison. After *Return to Peyton Place* was cancelled, Gallison moved over to *Days*. When it came time to find him a love interest, the producers remembered Frann's work on *Return to Peyton Place* and her chemistry with Gallison. She was hired to originate the role of Amanda Howard.

Had it been up to Deidre Hall, the show never would have hired Wayne Northrop as Roman Brady. Although he turned out to be one of her most popular leading men, after Hall screen-tested with Northrop, she found "absolutely no chemistry" between them. Executive producer Al Rabin, on the other hand, saw a spark between them that could grow into something more. In time, Hall and the audience recognized it as well.

James Reynolds was not at all the type the producers were looking for when they were casting the role of police officer Abe Carver. They saw the character as much older, a settled-down, married kind of guy. As such, they didn't even want to let Reynolds audition. After striking out with every actor in Hollywood that they thought might be right for the role, the producers finally agreed to let Reynolds read. They were so impressed with his audition that they altered the role to better fit him.

Kristian Alfonso was amazed that the producers hired her to play the role of Hope Williams. She didn't believe herself to be a good actress. So insecure was she that when the producers asked her to come in and screen-test with potential Bos, she panicked. Not having yet taped her first scene, she worried that the producers would realize she wasn't any good and fire her before her first day. So she instructed her agent to tell the producers that she couldn't help them out with their Bo search because she was in New York.

Peter Reckell grew a beard six weeks before coming in to read for the part of Bo Brady. When the producers suggested that he shave it off and remove his earring before the screen test, he told them that he needed the beard for another role for which he was being considered. Reckell landed the part anyway and the producers accepted the facial hair as a fitting look for the rebellious character he was playing. That look, in fact, became an often imitated trademark among soap characters in the mid-1980s.

Peter Reckell (Bo Brady) refused to shave off his beard for his screen test.

Arleen Sorkin (CALLIOPE JONES) was told by one New York casting director that she would never find work on the soaps. She had a definite "in" with *Days*, however, rooming with one of the show's producers, Shelly Curtis.

Mary Beth Evans (KAYLA BRADY) was not at all pleased by her screen test with future leading man Stephen Nichols (STEVE "PATCH" JOHNSON). For the test, Evans and Nichols acted out a particularly intense scene. When it was over, Evans walked away, commenting on her performance, "That was shit." In addition to auditioning for Kayla, Evans, who had recently bought a house with her new husband, also applied for a waitressing job. She put off going to pick up her uniform until she heard whether or not she'd gotten the role of Kayla.

After Darby Hinton read for the role of Melissa's probation officer, Ian Griffith, the producers asked him if he would be willing to shave off his mustache for the part. Since he wasn't sure that he even wanted the role, he told them he would not. Forty-five minutes later, he was offered the part.

The day that Drake Hogestyn auditioned for the role of Roman Brady, he was in a pretty bad mood. He wanted to just go in and get the whole thing over with. As he started to walk up the steps at the studio, he realized that if he wanted the role, he was going to have to lose his attitude. At first, the producers didn't think that he was the right age to be taking over the role. They were looking for someone a little bit older. At the time he auditioned, Hogestyn happened to be reading the Robert Ludlum espionage novel, *The Bourne Identity*, whose plotline paralleled that of the role he was auditioning for, an amnesiac spy. Despite the producers' initial hesitations, Hogestyn landed the role. He then called his mother and told her that he'd gotten a part on *One Life to Live*.

Billy Warlock's (FRANKIE BRADY) work on the short-lived serial *Capitol* made the *Days* producers realize that he was going to be a hot property. They signed him to a three-year contract before they had even come up with a character for him to play.

Years before, the producers had offered a contract to John Stamos, whose potential for popularity they recognized from his recurring role on *General Hospital*. Stamos's agent used the contract offer from *Days* to get Stamos boosted from recurring to contract status on *GH*.

After Judi Evans was hired to play Adrienne Johnson, the producers told her to lose some weight. It was the same thing she'd heard after being hired by *Guiding Light* and the same thing she would hear again after being hired by *Another World*.

In 1984, Jane Elliot turned down the role of Augusta Lockridge on *Santa Barbara* because she did not want to live in California. (Louise Sorel ended up with the part.) Several years later, the Los Angeles-based *Days* had better luck with Elliot because she happened to be going through a divorce at the time. She took the role of Anjelica Deveraux mainly to get her mind off of her personal problems.

The role of reporter Diana Colville was originally intended to be a short-term part, lasting perhaps a couple of weeks. That all changed when the show landed Genie Francis, who had made soap opera history as half of *General Hospital*'s Luke and Laura. She accepted the role on a Friday afternoon and taped her first scene on Monday morning. Over the weekend, the writers burned the midnight oil building up the role to something that could last more than a couple of weeks.

Derya Ruggles was hired as Dr. Robin Jacobs, a love interest for Dr. Mike Horton, then played by Michael T. Weiss. Mike and Robin's romance was complicated by their religious differences: Mike was Christian and Robin was Jewish. In the actors' real lives, the religions were reversed: Ruggles is Christian and Weiss Jewish.

A better actress than Charlotte Ross could not have been found to play the role of Shane Donovan's long-lost daughter, Eve. Not only did Ross create a sympathetic villainess in Eve, she also bore a striking resemblance to Jane Windsor, who had played Shane's ex-wife, Emma. Despite the strong physical similarity between Ross and Windsor, both blondes, the writers decided to reveal that Shane's fellow spy Gabrielle Pascal, played by the brunette Karen Moncrieff, was actually Eve's mother. Making that plot twist even less credible, Moncrieff herself was only five years older than Ross. Moncrieff saw Ross right before she screen-tested for Gabrielle and told herself that there was no way she was being hired to play Ross's mother.

When the show was looking for an actor to play the role of Cal Winters, they brought a number of hopefuls into the same room to read for the part. Wortham Krimmer, who would end up with the role, didn't want his performance to be influenced by anything the other actors did, so while the actors ahead of him did their readings, Krimmer turned his back to them and covered his ears.

Richard Biggs could not get the day off from work when *Days* was auditioning actors for the role of Dr. Marcus Hunter. At the time, he was handling telephone complaints for a waste disposal company in Los Angeles. The producers didn't find anyone they liked during that first audition, so they held another. Not wanting to miss a second opportunity, Biggs made up an excuse to get out of work. The producers liked him and called him back in several times, which meant coming up with a series of lies to tell his employer. By the time the final audition rolled around, Biggs had simply run out of plausible stories, so he decided to be up front with his boss. He admitted that he needed the day off to audition for a role on a soap opera. The boss rewarded his honesty by threatening to fire him if he walked out the door. Biggs quit his job in order to go to the audition and luckily never needed to go back.

For years after Deidre Hall left the show in 1987, the producers were eager to get her back. When it looked as though Hall might never return, they approached her real-life twin, Andrea Hall-Lovell (who had played Marlena's twin, Samantha), about taking on the role of Marlena.

After roles on primetime serials such as *Dallas* and *Dynasty*, J. Eddie Peck (HAWK HAWKINS) was doing so well with his primetime career that his agents were turning down offers from the daytime soaps. Gene Palumbo, who was head-writing *Days* at the time, was especially impressed with Peck's turn as the psychopathic, drug addicted Tommy McKay on *Dallas*, and specifically requested that he come in to read for the role of Hawk. One of the factors that motivated Peck to take the job was that the studio where *Days* is taped was not far from his house.

While in an acting class, Camilla Scott (MELISSA HORTON) heard another student mention that she was auditioning for *Days of Our Lives* the following day. When the student added that the role required singing, a bell went off in Scott's head. Just the previous night, she had been telling her boyfriend that if she was going to break into soaps, it would have to be with a singing role. She immediately contacted her agent, who got her into the audition. The producers asked her if she could sing. When she answered that she could, they asked, "Can you *really* sing?" She gave them a sample and was working three days later.

When Crystal Chappell screen-tested for the role of Carly Manning with Peter Reckell, the producers told him to ask her for her bra size. Not only did Chappell tell him, she bounced a few questions of her own back at him. Their bantering helped Chappell land the role.

When Robert Mailhouse read for the role of Lawrence Alamain, he took what was written as a serious scene and turned it into a comic moment. The producers found his interpretation hysterical and considered rewriting Lawrence as a comic villain. Then Michael Sabatino walked in and blew them away with his interpretation of Lawrence as the character had originally been conceived. Mailhouse, however, did not walk away empty-handed. He was hired to play police officer Brian Scofield, a role that allowed him a great deal of room for levity.

The first time Robert Kelker-Kelly came in to discuss replacing Peter Reckell as Bo Brady, the meeting was quite informal. He discussed the character with the producers and read a scene with Crystal Chappell, who played Bo's then love interest Carly Manning. Six weeks later, the producers gave him a script to memorize for his formal audition the next week. The day before the audition, Kelker-Kelly received a phone call from the studio telling him that he had been given the wrong script. As a result, he had less than twenty-four hours to memorize the right script, which included a page-long monologue.

Roberta Leighton was taking a trip through Eastern Europe when she received a fax describing the character of Ginger Dawson. Leighton wanted the part so badly that she cut her trip short and hopped on a twenty-two-hour flight back to Los Angeles to get to the audition in time.

Bryan Dattilo did push-ups to relieve his tension while waiting to read for the part of Lucas Roberts. During the three hours he waited, he did a lot of push-ups—so many that by the time he finally went in to read his face was totally red. For luck, Dattilo carried his mother's rosary beads in his pocket. He would have done so his first day on the job as well, but there was no pocket in the skin-color tights he wore in his very first scene. (Lucas was supposed to be naked in the scene.)

When Jaime Lyn Bauer came in to read for the role of Laura Horton, she wore very simple clothes. Laura, she figured, had spent the last seventeen years of her life catatonic in a mental hospital. The producers, on the other hand, suggested that when she come back, she fix up her hair and wear something nicer.

Roark Critchlow learned that he had won the role of Dr. Mike Horton while in the hospital with his wife Maria, who was giving birth to their second daughter. It was the second time he went up for the role. Back in the mid-1980s, he'd lost out to Michael T. Weiss.

While Tanya Boyd was auditioning for the role of Celeste, casting director Fran Bascom asked whether or not she could do an accent. Not wanting to lose the role, Boyd said that she could. She came up with Celeste's accent while watching *Rocky and Bullwinkle*, modeling her accent after Natasha (as in Boris and Natasha). When she went back in to read again, she learned that the producers were specifically looking for a Cajun

Producers advised Jaime Lyn Bauer (far right, pictured here with Krista Allen-Moritt and Alison Sweeney) to jazz up her hair and outfit for her screen test.

accent. Since she had never done a Cajun accent, she mixed a little French into the Natasha voice she'd come up with.

When Melissa Reeves left the show abruptly in 1995, the producers scrambled to find a replacement. By the time lookalike actress Stephanie Cameron was hired, the show was more than a week behind schedule. In her first five days on the job, Cameron had to tape eleven days' worth of episodes.

Victor Alfieri was the textbook example of a struggling actor when he auditioned for the role of Franco Kelly. He didn't even have a decent pair of pants to wear to the audition; he had to borrow a pair from his cousin. After he landed the role, he not only returned his cousin's pants, he bought him a new pair as well.

When Adam Caine heard that *Days* was casting the role of an Englishman, he assumed that the role would be yet another James Bond clone. After reading the script, he realized that Edmund P. Crumb was closer to Austin Powers than James Bond. When Caine checked out the show, he noticed that Susan Banks, who would be Edmund's love interest, wore glasses. Caine therefore brought a pair to wear during his own audition.

Julianne Morris received a call at 10:15 in the morning congratulating her on landing the role of Swamp Girl and instructing her to get to the studio by noon to begin work.

Missed Opportunities

DEIDRE HALL (DR. MARLENA EVANS) was up for two of primetime's biggest roles in the 1980s—Krystle Carrington on *Dynasty* and Maddie Hayes on *Moonlighting*. Although she wanted both badly, she learned afterward that the *Dynasty* producers had really wanted Linda Evans all along. Aaron Spelling, who executive produced *Dynasty* and produces a slew of primetime network serials, has subsequently gone on record naming Deidre Hall as the one daytime star he would most like to steal away. The *Moonlighting* role, of course, went to Cybill Shepherd.

In the mid-1980s, NBC wanted Melissa Reeves for a movie of the week entitled *Cinderella Summer*. Unfortunately for Reeves, *Days* could not spare her. Had she been able to swing it, Reeves would have ended up working opposite her future leading man, Billy Warlock (FRANKIE BRADY).

The role of Kelly Bundy on the long-running Fox sitcom *Married . . . with Children* came down to a choice between Charlotte Ross (EVE DONOVAN) and Christina Applegate. The producers picked Applegate, who had appeared on *Days* as a baby.

After starring with Richard Dean Anderson on the drama series *Seven Brides for Seven Brothers*, Drake Hogestyn (JOHN BLACK) found himself competing against his former castmate for the lead role in a pilot. The producers told both men not to worry—whomever didn't get this pilot would be cast in another one, by the name of *MacGyver*. While Hogestyn landed the pilot that crashed, Anderson became a household name as action hero MacGyver.

Shelley Long, who hails from the same Indiana hometown as Drake Hogestyn, wanted Hogestyn to play her husband in the 1998 WB sitcom *Kelly Kelly*. Hogestyn agreed on the condition that he be able to keep his *Days* job. When the two schedules couldn't be worked out, Robert Hays of *Airplane!* was hired as Long's husband. As it turned out, Hogestyn's decision was a wise one—*Kelly Kelly* lasted only a few weeks.

Bryan Dattilo and his sister Kristin, who acts as well, were up for the roles of Brandon and Brenda Walsh on the Fox teen serial *Beverly Hills, 90210*.

The producers of *Friends* toyed with the idea of hiring John Aniston to play father to his real-life daughter Jennifer Aniston, who stars on the show as Rachel Green. The role ultimately went to Ron Leibman.

The Actors Who Got Away

BACK IN THE EARLY 1980s, future movie star and Oscar-winning director Kevin Costner (*Dances with Wolves*) auditioned for the role of Chris Kositchek's brother Jake. Although the producers liked him and recognized his talent, they didn't feel that he was right for the role of Jake, who would later be revealed to be the Salem Strangler. Costner is but one of the many film or television actors who have been turned down for roles on *Days*.

Future Emmy winner Heather Tom (VICTORIA NEWMAN, *The Young and the Restless*) auditioned for the role of Sarah Horton.

Kurt McKinney auditioned for the part of Justin Kiriakis. He lost the role to Wally Kurth, who later took over the role of Ned Ashton on *General Hospital* from McKinney, who moved on to play *Guiding Light's* Matt Reardon.

Ellen Wheeler (VICKY and MARLEY LOVE, *Another World*; CINDY CHANDLER, *All My Children*) was an established actress with two Emmys to her credit when she read for the part of psychiatrist Whitney Baker, a role that was recast twice within a couple of months before ultimately being abandoned.

Prior to landing the role of Wheeler's father on *Another World*, Kale Browne tested for the part of John Black. His *Days* audition actually helped him land the job at *Another World*.

Wally Kurth, pictured here with wife Rena Sofer,
won the role of Justin Kiriakis over Kurt McKinney,
whom he later replaced on *General Hospital*.

Adrian Zmed, who had acted on *T. J. Hooker* and hosted *Dance Fever,* came very close to landing the role of Hawk Hawkins.

When the role of Kate Roberts was being brought back to the show, several name actresses were considered for the part, including Lois Chiles (James Bond's love interest in *Moonraker* and one of J. R. Ewing's many women on *Dallas*); Deborah Shelton (another of J. R.'s love interests), and Janice Lynde, who had played Jaime Lyn Bauer's sister on *The Young and the Restless.*

Sean Kanan auditioned for the part of Austin. Instead he landed on *General Hospital* as A. J. Quartermaine, a role later taken over by Billy Warlock (FRANKIE BRADY).

Alla Korot, who went on to play Dr. Alison Doyle on *All My Children,* tried out for the role of Billie Reed when it was being recast. When *Days* was recasting Austin Reed, Michael Lowry (DR. JAKE MARTIN, *All My Children*) tried out for the role. Instead of playing brother and sister on *Days,* Korot and Lowry ended up playing lovers on *All My Children.*

Several actors have tried out for one role and ended up with another. Among them: Susan Diol, who auditioned for Carly Manning, but ended up with the role of Carly's romantic rival Emmy Borden; Miriam Parrish, who tried out for Sami Brady and ended up as her best friend Jamie Caldwell; and Matt Battaglia, who went up for Bo Brady when it was being recast, but years later was brought on as Bo's drug dealing nemesis, King.

On Their Way Out

CATHERINE MARY STEWART, who originated the role of Kayla Brady, had a clause written into her contract allowing her time off to pursue outside projects, such as primetime and feature film work. After the third time she exercised that clause, the producers decided to let her go.

Seeing the unceremonious way in which Jed Allan (DON CRAIG) was written off *Days* without so much as a proper send off for the character prompted Thaao Penghlis (TONY DIMERA) to leave the show in 1985. Penghlis himself wanted a very dramatic end to his storyline, having Tony die in his beloved wife Anna's arms. Instead, he disappeared into the fog one night.

Michael Sabatino (LAWRENCE ALAMAIN) realized that he was being let go when he heard over the loudspeaker Thaao Penghlis being paged to one of the producer's offices. Although Sabatino had not worked with Penghlis on the show, he knew enough about his character, a suave but shady European millionaire, to realize that there wasn't going to be room for Lawrence Alamain if Tony DiMera was being brought back.

After Jane Elliot left the role of Anjelica Deveraux, the show wanted Judith Chapman, who had wowed audiences as Ginny Webber on *General Hospital,* to take over the role. Chapman was unavailable, so her former castmate Shelley Taylor Morgan was hired. A few weeks later, when Chapman became available, Morgan was fired. All along, Morgan knew that her *Days* days were numbered. As she told *Soap Opera Digest*, she knew that she didn't look old enough to play the older woman to Wally Kurth (JUSTIN KIRIAKIS).

Judi Evans (ADRIENNE JOHNSON KIRIAKIS) did not leave *Days* over a salary dispute or to try her luck in primetime and feature films. She moved East to spend more time with her husband. Unfortunately that marriage ended in divorce.

At one point, the producers approached Billy Hufsey (EMILIO RAMIREZ) about cutting his hair, which at the time he was wearing shoulder length. When Hufsey refused to cut his hair, explaining that he needed to keep it long for his music career, he found his character being written off the show. Negative fan reaction to Hufsey's departure pushed the show to hire him back.

In the late 1980s, Frank Parker (SHAWN BRADY), complained to one soap opera magazine about the show's obsession with younger storylines to the exclusion of the older characters. Shortly after the comments appeared in print, Parker's agent received a phone call from one of the show's producers telling him that Parker would not be working on the show any longer. It wasn't until a new regime came in a year later that Parker was rehired.

When Peter Reckell chose to leave *Days* for the second time in 1991, he expressed his disapproval that the show was planning to recast the role of Bo Brady.

Camilla Scott (MELISSA HORTON) first heard that she was being let go not from anyone at the show but from a friend who followed all the back-stage gossip.

On her seventeenth birthday, Christie Clark (CARRIE BRADY) learned that the show was letting her go in order to age the character. She was brought back two years later after the producers determined that she looked old enough to be playing romantic scenes.

Deborah Adair (KATE ROBERTS) left the show in 1995 to concentrate her energy on starting a family. A year later, she and her husband, *Melrose Place* producer Chip Hayes, adopted a baby girl.

Staci Greason (ISABELLA TOSCANO BLACK) left *Days* because she had simply gotten sick of acting.

Backstage Pass

DEIDRE HALL AND WAYNE NORTHROP (MARLENA EVANS and ROMAN BRADY) became infamous around the *Days* set for the practical jokes they would play on each other. Before one scene in which Northrop was to jump into bed, Hall soaked the sheets. Although Northrop finished the scene as though nothing was wrong, as soon as the cameras stopped rolling, he threw a fully costumed Hall into the shower. Another time, Hall threw a bucket of water on Northrop during a scene where he was just about to say, "I need a shower." Northrop, in turn, tied the door to her dressing room shut so tightly that prop men were summoned to get her out to do her scene.

The first day that Wes Kenney arrived at the NBC studios to begin producing *Days,* he noticed that the name in his parking spot had been misspelled *Kenny.* Since his last name had been misspelled so often during his life, he had become a bit defensive about the correct spelling. He not only asked the people in charge to change it, he added for incentive that if it wasn't changed by the time he arrived at work the next day, he would be driving right back out the gate.

Brian Autenrieth, who played Zachary, the boy Megan Hathaway was passing off as Bo Brady's son, idolized Peter Reckell (BO BRADY). So great was Autenrieth's devotion that his mother had to buy him a trademark Bo Brady outfit—khaki pants, motorcycle gloves, and a red bandanna.

Peter Reckell stays in shape by riding his bike to work.

Reckell's replacement, Robert Kelker-Kelly, used to memorize his lines each day by pecking them out on a typewriter.

Patricia Barry (ADDIE HORTON) used to memorize her lines by recording them. Blessed with a photographic memory, she would literally memorize the page as she recorded it. On her way into work each morning, she would listen to the tape. By the time she got to the studio, she knew not only her own lines but her castmates' as well.

Wally Kurth's first job at *Days of Our Lives* was not playing Justin Kiriakis; it was printing up cue cards in the late 1970s.

As a child actor, Lisa Trusel (MELISSA HORTON) found it difficult to balance school and work. At one point, she went to the producers and asked them to hire her a private tutor for the set, but they refused, claiming it would cost too much. By the time finals rolled around, the fourteen-year-old Trusel felt as though she was on the verge of a nervous breakdown. When the tension began to take away from her performance, the producers found the money for a tutor.

When Philece Sampler learned that her character, Renée Dumonde, was to be done in by the Salem Slasher, she decided to throw herself a going away party. As a joke she had a photo taken of herself in a coffin.

Charles Shaughnessy (SHANE DONOVAN) hated the job he did his first day on the job. He was so disgusted by his performance that he went home and drank himself sick.

In 1988, Kayla Brady (Mary Beth Evans) was temporarily deafened during a fight with the Riverfront Knifer. After regaining her hearing, she and new husband Steve Johnson (Stephen Nichols) became involved in the plight of a young deaf boy. Within a mere two weeks, Evans and Nichols had learned enough sign language to do their scenes.

When Christie Clark (CARRIE BRADY) was working on the show as a child, she had a nifty trick for crying on camera. Right before the time came for tears, she would simply tell herself that if she didn't cry, she would lose her job.

Christie Clark (CARRIE BRADY)
developed a trick for crying on cue.

Patsy Pease's second pregnancy was written into the show. Her character, Kimberly, worried that she might be carrying madman Cal Winters's child. Pease worried how the storyline might affect her real-life pregnancy, which was already considered high risk. She had not felt comfortable playing out a miscarriage storyline while pregnant with her first son, Joshua. On the advice of her doctor, Pease requested a medical leave for the remainder of her second pregnancy. When she would occasionally tune in to the show and watch her replacement, Anne Howard, tangle with Wortham Krimmer as Cal Winters, Pease was very happy not to be playing those scenes. She subsequently gave birth to a healthy son, Russell.

Anne Howard, who filled in for Patsy Pease as Kimberly Brady Donovan, could not stand using cue cards. Nor could she stand her leading man, Charles Shaughnessy (SHANE DONOVAN), relying on them. So, as a wedding present to her, Shaughnessy promised that he would give them up.

The dentist that Michael Sabatino went to as a child was notorious for never giving his patients novocaine or painkillers of any variety. Sabatino based his characterization of the ruthless and at times sadistic millionaire Lawrence Alamain on that dentist.

One time, the prop people forgot to clear away the stale bread that was used on the set of the Brady Fish Market. During the night, the scent attracted a swarm of rats who ate not only the bread but enough pieces of the set itself that a new fish market set needed to be built.

While actresses are famous for bleaching their hair to win a role, Shannon Sturges (MOLLY BRINKER) actually went the other way. The show had so many young blondes (among them Melissa Reeves and Charlotte Ross) when she joined the cast that she was instructed to dye her naturally blonde hair brunette.

For one scene, producer Shelly Curtis simply wasn't pleased with anything the wardrobe department was offering up for Kristian Alfonso to wear as Hope. Just before the scene was to commence taping, Curtis ran home and raided her own closet for an appropriate outfit.

When trouble began brewing between Dr. Marlena Evans and the middle class Stella Lombard, the producers were not satisfied with Stella's wardrobe. They wanted to play up the visual differences between Marlena and Stella by dressing Stella down—way down. Unfortunately, none of the clothes in wardrobe really captured the look that the producers were going after. Everything looked too good, too classy. The next day, Elaine Bromka, who played Stella, brought in a collection of clothes, which the producers loved, deciding that they were dowdy enough. When they asked Bromka where she had found them, Bromka admitted that they were her own clothes.

The day that Days taped the scene in which Vivian Alamain buried Carly Manning alive, a local television station was airing a repeat of the Tom Selleck series Magnum, P.I. in which Magnum was buried alive. As a joke, a cameraman who discovered the show was on, broadcast the repeat on all the monitors around the studio. Taking a cue from that, Crystal Chappell snuck a baseball bat, cap, and fake mustache into the coffin with her. She emerged from the coffin at the end of the scene dressed as Tom Selleck.

Ever the prankster, Michael Sabatino (LAWRENCE ALAMAIN) once walked into the studio completely naked.

Patrick Muldoon (AUSTIN REED) was understandably shocked when Macdonald Carey, who'd been with the show from the first episode, asked Patrick's permission to change a line of dialogue in a scene they were doing together.

Roark Critchlow (DR. MIKE HORTON) refuses to run lines with any of his female costars behind closed doors.

During the Maison Blanche storyline, in which Stefano DiMera imprisoned John Black in his dungeon, Drake Hogestyn went on a very strict diet to get into the proper mood and physical condition. In three weeks, he lost twenty pounds. The show, of course, had doctors monitoring his weight and health.

Peggy McCay (CAROLINE BRADY), who was raised Catholic, helped Drake Hogestyn sharpen the terminology in his dialogue after his character,

John Black, discovered that he was really a priest. McCay's cousin, a priest, helped the show locate an expert on exorcism during the Satanic possession storyline.

The Satanic possession storyline had a few people on the set a bit freaked out at times. One scene called for the chair Caroline Brady was sitting on to rattle. When it did, one cue card holder dropped his cards.

Different actors on the set had their own ways of dealing with the possession storyline. McCay would not do any of the Satanic scenes unless she was wearing both her crucifix and her St. Michael's medal. Drake Hogestyn and Deidre Hall, the two actors most deeply invested in the story, said a prayer together in the corner before each of their scenes.

The avalanche scene in Aremid that buried Hope Williams (Kristian Alfonso) was supposed to have been filmed on location in Utah. When time ran short, the producers decided to tape inside the studio. Ironically, it took the director less time to tape the avalanche itself than to get a decent shot of Hope's hand coming up through the snow.

After Krista Allen-Moritt's first week on the air as Billie Reed, she received a delivery of flowers at the studio from Lisa Rinna, who had originated the role. The card attached read: "Congratulations. I think you are perfect as the new Billie. I hope you have as much fun with her as I did."

During the storyline in the French underground, John Black was sentenced to death by guillotine. The blade in that guillotine was not a fake; it was very real and very sharp. A memo was sent to all the cast and crew members telling them to stay away from it.

While reading the breakdowns on upcoming storylines, Louise Sorel saw the name Don Craig mentioned several times, so she called up to tell her friend and former *Santa Barbara* castmate Jed Allan, who had played Don for fourteen years. He was very excited at the idea of returning to the show. After some time had passed without any contact from *Days*, Allan placed a call to his former leading lady, Deidre Hall, to see if she could tell him what was going on. Hall spoke to executive producer Tom Langan.

As it turned out, the name Don Craig had been used as a ruse in the breakdowns so that word wouldn't leak out that the show was actually bringing back Marlena's other husband, Roman Brady. Allan was understandably disappointed, especially since the misunderstanding came on the heels of a similar disappointment at *Sunset Beach*—after being all but promised the patriarch role, he learned that the show was going with another actor.

Eileen Davidson proved herself to be one real chameleon when she took on her second *Days* role, that of the buck-toothed, badly dressed Susan Banks. Her getup as Susan even managed to fool executive producer Tom Langan, who walked right by her in the hallway and asked one of the production assistants why such an unattractive extra had been hired.

Tom Langan suggested to Davidson that to better affect Susan's lisp, she should stick bubble gum to the roof of her mouth.

One of Eileen Davidson's biggest challenges in her parade of multiple characters was pulling off that of gangster Thomas Banks. More than simply acting the role, Davidson made suggestions on how to most effectively transform her into a man. In an effort to hide her slender neck, Davidson requested a neck piece that she could wear underneath a turtleneck sweater. She also suggested that a long wig would help. Although she initially resisted the idea of using a voice modifier, believing that she could simply lower her voice on her own, she admitted that the device, which not only lowered her voice but also changed the timbre of it, worked out for the best.

One of Eileen Davidson's scenes as Sister Mary Moira Banks originally called for her to rap the troublemaking Sami Brady on the knuckles with a ruler. Davidson, who had gone through the parochial school system, knew that nuns no longer rap knuckles with rulers, so she had the scene rewritten. Sister Mary Moira still carried the ruler, but she assured Sami's mother Marlena that nuns don't hit people with them anymore.

Hazards of the Job

PETER RECKELL BROKE his hand in two places during a fight scene between Bo Brady and Russian agents. Reckell didn't realize that he had broken it until some time later, when the throbbing refused to stop. Because Bo didn't break his hand, Reckell had to be outfitted with a removable cast.

During an early fight scene between Bo and John Black, Drake Hogestyn accidentally elbowed Peter Reckell right in the face. Reckell's lip swelled, and he ended up with some scar tissue inside his mouth. Not one to believe in accidents, Reckell told *Soap Opera Digest* that he held that misplay against Hogestyn for some time. Reckell believed that it might have been the newcomer Hogestyn's way of one-upping the show's reigning hero.

Peter Reckell found that it wasn't just the fight scenes that could prove hazardous to his health. He had his share of problems filming love scenes as well. While doing one bedroom scene with Kristian Alfonso (HOPE), Reckell leaned over to turn on the light and ended up falling on the floor. He landed on the lamp cord, which brought the lamp down on top of him. Alfonso ended up on top of him on the floor as well. Another time, Kristian Alfonso accidentally hit Reckell in the groin during a love scene. And Reckell, also unintentionally, bit Alfonso's lip when Bo went to kiss Hope.

Although Peter Reckell and Stephen Nichols never stabbed each other during the knife fights between Patch and Bo, Nichols was always worried that one of them, probably himself, would slip up. He was a little unnerved by the fact that the prop people had given them real knives and that the eye patch he wore as Patch took away his sense of depth perception.

As Jack and Jennifer were walking up the aisle after getting married, Matthew Ashford walked straight into a door.

During the storyline in which Carrie was filming a vampire movie at the Alamain house, a fire hose went out of control. As soon as the water was turned on, it proved to be too much for the extras holding the hose. The set was flooded and production stalled for a number of hours.

The wardrobing demands for Pat Delaney's portrayal of burn victim Rachel Blake (aka the Lady in White) required her to wear a lace veil over her head for months on end. The audience could not see Delaney's face, and Delaney herself was all but walking blind. She often missed her mark and ended up walking into the furniture.

While taping a fight scene with Kristian Alfonso, Jeff Griggs (JUDE ST. CLAIR) accidentally hit her in the jaw, causing her to see stars. At first, she worried that the blow had broken her jaw. When it was determined that the jaw was not broken, the scene continued.

When Kristian Alfonso first auditioned for the role of Hope, she tripped and fell down the flight of stairs in the Horton house.

In 1993, Frances Reid (ALICE HORTON) fell on the set and dislocated her shoulder. The accident did not, however, cause her to miss a single day of work.

One scene called for a frustrated Carrie Brady (Christie Clark) to finally haul off and slap Sami (Alison Sweeney) right across the face. During the rehearsal, Clark asked Sweeney for permission to make physical contact with the slap. The two actresses practiced several times before it came time to tape. During the taping, Clark was standing closer to Sweeney than she had during the rehearsal. As a result, the slap not only connected with Sweeney's face, it knocked her to the ground. In falling, Sweeney hit her head on the piano. Unfortunately for the director, Sweeney swore so much after being hit that the footage could not be used.

Alison Sweeney brought on her own problems while filming scenes in which Sami was to give birth to her son Will. While rehearsing, she did the Lamaze breathing techniques she'd studied in preparation for the labor scenes. She did them again during the dress rehearsal. While doing the Lamaze breathing a third time during the actual taping, a now dizzy Sweeney began hyperventilating.

Accidents don't just happen on the set or involve merely the actors. When Irna Phillips, who helped to create the show, was attending a story meeting, a painting fell off the wall and hit her in the head. Although nurses came in to look at her, Phillips, a notorious hypochondriac, was rushed to a nearby hospital, where it was determined that she was fine.

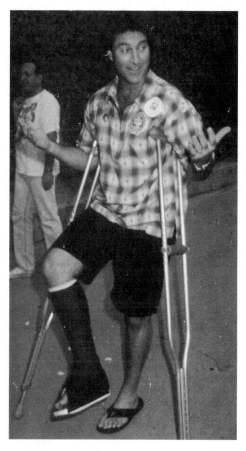

Like many of his castmates, Drake Hogestyn (JOHN BLACK) has learned to play hurt.

Clash of the Titans

ALTHOUGH BO AND HOPE were the most popular couple on daytime television in the mid-1980s, the relationship between their portrayers, Peter Reckell and Kristian Alfonso, was less than congenial. Tension between the two was so great that they refused to go to the same public appearances together. Alfonso came close to quitting the show several times because of negative comments Reckell had made in the press about her.

Ironically, Kristian Alfonso had an even harder time getting along with Reckell's replacement, Robert Kelker-Kelly. According to Michael Logan's column in *TV Guide,* Alfonso had refused to re-sign with the show unless it fired Robert Kelker-Kelly, who was playing Bo to her Hope/Gina. Shortly thereafter, Kelker-Kelly was out of a job and Peter Reckell was back as Bo. By this time, it should be noted, the tension between Alfonso and Reckell had evolved into friendship. Once Kelker-Kelly was fired, his two previous leading ladies, Crystal Chappell and Lisa Rinna, made some veiled comments to *Soap Opera Digest,* alluding to a troubled history with the actor.

Peter Reckell also managed to get off on the wrong foot with Crystal Chappell, his first leading lady after Kristian Alfonso left the show in 1990. His criticism of Chappell's acting abilities drove her to the point of tears. After she got past that, she decided to learn what she could from him and considers herself a better actress for the discussions they had.

Although Robert S. Woods (BO BUCHANAN, *One Life to Live*) was eager to join *Days* in the mid- to late-1980s, he does not look back with fondness at the experience or his relationship with the show's then producer, Al Rabin. "I'd rather say nothing than tell you what I really think of him," Woods told *Soap Opera Digest* in the May 3, 1988 cover story. According to Woods, he felt as if he may have been "forced down Rabin's throat," hired because of his name when another actor had already been chosen for the part of Paul Stewart. Rabin responded to the forced hiring by using Woods as little as possible.

By 1980, the tension between Susan Seaforth Hayes and Brenda Benet, who played Julie's onscreen rival Lee Dumonde, had reached the breaking point. Not only was Lee keeping Doug from Julie, Benet herself developed feelings for her leading man, Bill Hayes, which didn't sit too well with Seaforth Hayes, his real-life spouse. As detailed in Jason Bonderoff's *Soap Opera Babylon,* the feud between the two actresses almost wound up in court. Benet wanted to have Seaforth Hayes charged with assault for hitting her in the face with a purse. Seaforth Hayes countered that the incident had happened within in the context of a scene. As for charges that Seaforth Hayes verbally abused her, Seaforth Hayes responded that the two of them did not even speak with one another. Executive producer Al Rabin intervened and got Benet to abandon the lawsuit.

Michael Easton, who played bad boy Tanner Scofield, found himself developing a reputation for being a bad boy off the set as well. He engaged in more than one battle with the higher-ups over the length of his hair. After cutting it once at the show's request, Easton decided not to do so again, no matter how much they asked. More than simply being obstinate, Easton refused to cut his hair because he didn't think that Tanner would just go out and get a stylish cut solely to make himself look better. Easton did, however, at producer Al Rabin's request, give up wearing a pair of tattered jeans even though he believed they fit the character. By the time Easton left the show, less than two years after he arrived, his bad boy attitude and antics—including walking off the set at one point—led

During their first go round as Hope and Bo, Kristian Alfonso and Peter Reckell made few public appearances together. (Also pictured on far left, Victor Alfieri)

to his being banned from the offices upstairs and forbidden to utter a four-letter obscenity anywhere in the studio.

When Deidre Hall returned to *Days* in the early 1990s, the tabloid newspapers reported that there was a feud going on between her and Crystal Chappell, who had become the show's leading lady in Hall's absence. While feud may have been a bit strong to describe the situation, there definitely was tension. At the time Hall returned, Chappell was going through a divorce that left her understandably unhappy. Hall blamed Chappell for letting her own unhappiness affect the studio. As a result, the women wound up speaking to each other as little as possible.

When Thaao Penghlis returned to *Days* in the mid-1990s, his character Tony DiMera was reintroduced as Kristen Blake's (Eileen Davidson) mystery fiancé. Despite the need for an immediate bond between their characters, Penghlis didn't connect on a personal level with Davidson. He told *Soap Opera Digest,* "We weren't totally cold, but Eileen is not easily accessible." Davidson herself had no idea how Penghlis felt until she read about trouble between them in the soap press. She brought it up to Penghlis, expecting him to laugh it off as nonsense. Instead, he told her how he felt.

Banned in Salem

DAYS OF OUR LIVES' first stab at a socially conscious storyline upset more than a few sponsors. In the ecologically minded late 1960s, a story about water pollution seemed, if nothing else, timely. When the source of the pollution was traced back to a company that manufactured soap, the show's advertisers, many of them soap companies, were up in arms. The storyline was immediately killed. Frances Reid (ALICE HORTON) remembered people coming up to her in the supermarket, asking what had happened to the story. Reid bluffed her way through those encounters, commenting that the fans must have missed the episode where the storyline was wrapped up.

Viewers might have found the romance between Marie Horton and Dr. Mark Brooks (Maree Cheatham and John Lupton) a tad on the reserved side. Even back in the 1960s, soap fans were accustomed to seeing some physical displays of affection between couples in love. But with Mark and Marie, there was none. Kisses and handholding may have been implied but were never seen on camera. The censors, who knew that Mark was going to turn out to be Marie's long-presumed-dead brother Tommy, could not allow a less than chaste kiss to take place onscreen between a brother and sister.

After successfully dancing around the issue of incest with the Marie/Tommy pairing, *Days* was set to explore yet another taboo: male rape. The storyline in which Bill Horton met Doug Williams in prison was scripted to include a scene in which the guards would bring a male inmate, who had been raped in the showers, into the infirmary. Just before the dress rehearsal, the actors and director received word from the higher-ups that the scene could not air as written. In the quickly revised scene, the inmate was brought into the infirmary after being beaten up, not raped. Making this story somewhat ironic, Bill Horton was in jail because of events that had transpired after he raped his sister-in-law.

The interracial romance between Valerie Grant, a black woman, and Julie Williams's son David Banning, a white man, was a tricky plotline from the start. The network was more than a little concerned about it, especially when it came time for the two characters to kiss onscreen. *Days* did not get approval from the higher-ups for that kiss until the very day that it was to be taped.

When the character of Justin Kiriakis (Wally Kurth) was introduced, he was quite the Romeo. Within his first few weeks on the show, he'd had sex with a woman in France, a flight attendant during the flight, and a maid in his uncle's mansion. He was also making his move on Melissa Jannings. Word came down from the network to tone down Justin's sexual antics. Later, when Justin began his affair with older woman Anjelica Deveraux, he pulled out a condom before making love to her. The scene, which aired in 1987, marked one of the first times that a condom had been shown on daytime television.

Head writer Thom Racina wanted to pen an AIDS storyline in 1987, but he was not allowed to do so.

In the 1992 primetime special, "One Stormy Night," Bo and Carly were scripted to be lying in bed kissing. Although scenes like that had been played out countless times during the afternoon, the censors considered it a bit much for the eight o'clock hour when the primetime special was scheduled to air. As a result, their kissing scene was altered to show them standing up.

Toward the end of Eileen Davidson's run on *Days*, her character, Kristen, was seen plotting with a mysterious turbaned man. As it turned out, Kristen had sold her lookalike Susan Banks into a harem. The storyline drew criticism from Arab American groups, who disapproved of the stereotypical portrayal of Arabs as harem lords. The groups contacted their local congressmen who in turn complained to General Electric, which owns NBC. NBC strongly suggested that *Days* change the storyline. That change required five shows to be completely re-taped. In the revamped version, the harem leaders were no longer Arabs. They were white men running an island compound. All the harem costumes and scenery the viewers had seen the week before were dismissed in a line of dialogue as part of a theme week the compound leaders had been celebrating.

While the censors shot down a scene depicting Anna sponging Tony's back in the shower, one rather risqué bathtub scene between Patch and Kayla shocked a few viewers when it aired in 1988. Patch and Kayla were facing each other from opposite ends of a tub. Kayla made some joke about snorkeling and submerged her head under the water in the direction of Patch's groin. The camera then focused in on Patch's face as it broke into a grin. It was one of daytime's most suggestive depictions of oral sex—all the more shocking because oral sex is seldom even spoken about on the afternoon soaps.

Charles Shaughnessy was surprised when one of his scripts called for Shane Donovan to refer to another character as a "nasty old bugger." While the term can mean simply any person of contempt, in England, where Shaughnessy comes from, the word *bugger* holds a much stronger definition (namely a sodomite), one that would not have gotten by the censors if they were better versed in British slang.

The Negotiating Table

FRANCES REID (ALICE HORTON) hates going out shopping for new cars. Thanks to *Days*, she doesn't need to. One of the perks written into her contract is that *Days of Our Lives* buys her a brand new car every other year.

Back when Pat Falken Smith was head-writing the show in the mid-1970s, she not only received a quarter million dollar base salary, she also received a $35,000 bonus for "thinking creatively."

At one point, contract negotiations were not going smoothly between *Days of Our Lives* and Quinn Redeker, who played the popular villain Alex Marshall. When both sides seemed to have come to a standstill, Alex was shot seven times. As Alex's life hung in the balance, Ken Corday told Redeker's agent that the rest of the negotiations would determine how close to Alex's brain any of those bullets had reached. Within twenty-four hours, the two sides reached an agreement.

Gloria Loring (LIZ CURTIS), who had a fairly successful musical career before coming to daytime, decided to capitalize on the immense popularity of her character. She negotiated a clause in her contract that not only allowed her time off to do outside projects but one that also guaranteed her outside work. NBC managed to fulfill its obligation by finding her guest spots on various of its primetime series. Negotiated in 1983, this sort of clause was a first for daytime actors.

When Drake Hogestyn (JOHN BLACK) came to the negotiating table several years ago, he had a very simple, although somewhat unusual, request.

With his heavy workload on the show, he found it hard finding time to get a haircut. So, in addition to the typical salary boosts and scheduling considerations, he wanted the show to arrange for someone to cut his hair every two weeks.

One of the main considerations Kristian Alfonso had when she agreed to come back to *Days* in 1994 was that she wanted to play Hope even though Hope had been "killed off" in an explosion when Alfonso left the show in 1990. Between 1990 and 1994, the show had approached Alfonso about coming back not as Hope but as a Hope lookalike. Alfonso wanted no part of that. When she agreed to come back in 1994, she not only wanted to play Hope, she wanted it guaranteed in writing.

J. Eddie Peck, whose character Hawk was introduced as a possible love interest for Jennifer Deveraux, believed that he was brought on mainly to force Matthew Ashford's (JACK DEVERAUX) cooperation during a difficult contract negotiation. As soon as Ashford signed his new contract, Peck found himself being written off the show.

One of the perks Thaao Penghlis received for returning to *Days* in the early 1990s was a twenty thousand dollar shopping spree in Rome and Milan for his character's wardrobe.

When Deidre Hall and Wayne Northrop returned to *Days* in 1991, their contracts were initially only for six months. One of the terms of those contracts was special billing during the end credits: "With special appearances by Wayne Northrop as Roman Brady and Deidre Hall as Marlena Evans."

It was Deidre Hall's contract, however, that drew the most attention from the media. Her salary was so hefty that Corday Productions went to NBC to ask the network to kick in some of the money it was costing to get her back. Hall was also supposed to be given the chance to executive produce a program of her own. Many felt that the program would be the proposed *Days* spin-off *Manhattan Lives,* but the spin-off never materialized.

Arousing the most attention was a clause in her contract that gave her a dressing room with its own shower. According to varied articles, Drake Hogestyn, whose dressing room was the only one in the studio with a shower, was evicted to accommodate Hall's request.

Deidre Hall's 1991 return to _Days_ earned her a number of contract perks.

Legal Dramas

AFTER LIFTING *Days* from the brink of cancellation to the top of the Nielsen ratings, Bill Bell became a hot property in daytime, so hot that CBS wanted him to create a soap opera for their network. The offer was just too tempting, and Bell decided to leave *Days* to create *The Young and the Restless.* Corday Productions responded by filing a lawsuit to prevent Bell from leaving. A settlement was reached out of court allowing Bell to create and head-write *The Young and the Restless* but requiring him to stay on at *Days* for three years as story editor.

According to Jason Bonderoff's *Soap Opera Babylon,* former head writer Pat Falken Smith sued NBC, Corday Productions, and Columbia Pictures for several million dollars after leaving the show amidst "a heated contract dispute." A couple years later, the lawsuit was dropped and Smith was back head-writing *Days,* though not for long.

Shortly after celebrating her tenth anniversary with the show, Melissa Reeves (JENNIFER HORTON DEVERAUX) quit, citing personal problems, even though she still had several months left on her contract. When word got back to Ken Corday a year later that Reeves was considering joining the cast of *General Hospital,* he filed a breach of contract suit preventing her from working anywhere but on *Days.* The court papers revealed that Reeves had left the show after her husband discovered that she'd been having an affair with a male costar. Although the name of that costar was not revealed in the court papers, the tabloid press and *Playgirl* magazine named Reeves's leading man Jason Brooks (PETER BLAKE) as her offscreen lover. Brooks denied the allegation and threatened to sue *Playgirl* but never did. The case against Reeves was eventually settled out of court in 1997 for an undisclosed amount of money.

Former *Days* actress Hunter Tylo (MARINA TOSCANO) recently won more than five million dollars in a lawsuit she filed against television producer Aaron Spelling. Spelling had offered Tylo a pivotal role on his primetime serial *Melrose Place*, then rescinded the offer after the contract was signed when Tylo revealed that she was pregnant. Spelling maintained that Tylo's pregnancy violated the clause in her contract forbidding her from changing her appearance. The *Melrose Place* role went to another *Days* alumna, Lisa Rinna (BILLIE REED), who herself became pregnant but was not fired.

In the last few years, Deidre Hall could easily win an award as most litigious soap star. In 1995, she sued the estate of her late therapist to recover $800,000 she had loaned him. The case was settled out of court for an undisclosed amount. The following year, she filed a suit against her accountant for embezzling $1.4 million from her. Most recently, she sued a former nanny, who penned an unflattering tell-all about Hall's family, as well as the book's publisher.

Postcards from the Road

THE SHOW'S FIRST LOCATION shoot outside of California took several cast members, most notably Bo and Hope (Peter Reckell and Kristian Alfonso) down to New Orleans. While Bo was in town trying to get his hands on one of the mystic prisms that Stefano DiMera was after, the romantic setting also provided the perfect backdrop for the romance between Bo and Hope, who made love for the very first time in the Oak Valley plantation house. The location shoot also gave the actors and behind-the-scenes crew a taste of how zealous the show's fans had become. When seven thousand people showed up at the airport to greet Reckell and Alfonso's arrival, the airport had to be temporarily shut down due to the crowds. Fans also managed to find out where Reckell was staying and literally chased him around his hotel.

A 1985 scavenger hunt storyline found Pete Jannings and Melissa Horton (Michael Leon and Lisa Trusel) and later Bo and Hope running around the country, trying to piece together the clues in a mysterious set of photographs. The show took to the road for the storyline. When *Days* landed in Boston, Mother Nature herself provided crowd control. A small hurricane cleared out historic Faneuil Hall on the day that *Days* filmed its scenes there. Later on, Bo and Hope headed to Miami. The producers had hoped to coordinate a crossover between the Miami leg of the storyline with the NBC primetime police drama, *Miami Vice*. Although those plans fell through, *Days* did copy *Miami Vice*'s music video style for one literally explosive cliffhanger.

The wedding of supercouple Bo and Hope demanded special attention. The show not only went on location, it went overseas for the first time, to England. In the storyline, Bo and Hope were treated to the wedding courtesy of the Royal Family as a thank you for thwarting an assassin who preyed upon royalty. Making the remote that much harder to shoot was a patch of truly unpredictable weather. One day started out overcast; after a bit of sun, the clouds returned and let loose a rainstorm. After another bit of sun, the clouds came back not for another rainstorm but rather a snowstorm.

The marriage of Adrienne Johnson and Justin Kiriakis (Judi Evans and Wally Kurth) brought *Days of Our Lives* to Greece, a remote that would never have been planned if the producers knew ahead of time that the Greek government would not allow them to tape anything but landscape shots. The government did not want any of the show's dramatic moments to be taped at historic sites. Too much time and money, however, had been invested in the remote for the show to simply walk away with only landscape footage. So producer Al Rabin got sneaky. While Evans and Kurth strolled around the ruins of the Temple of Poseidon reciting their dialogue, a technician with a hidden mini-cam recorded their every movement. A guard grew suspicious watching Johnson, Kurth, and the man following them. Despite Rabin's attempts at distraction, the guard figured out what was happening and ordered them all to leave the area. By that time, the show had luckily accumulated enough footage to justify the trip. Scenes at the Acropolis and the Parthenon had to be similarly taped on the sly.

John Black's search for his true identity, coupled with Marlena Evans and Roman Brady's quest to find out the reason behind their years of captivity, took them—along with Roman's brother Bo and his lady love Carly Manning—down to the Mayan Pyramid in Chichen Itza, Mexico. While the weather affected the remotes in Boston and England, the producers lucked out in Mexico. During the entire week of taping, Hurricane Fabian swirled around just off the coast but never touched down on land.

The main difficulty with the shoot concerned the pyramid itself. There were ninety-one narrow steps from the base of the pyramid to the top. The scene in which Bo and Carly walked the entire way up took five hours to tape—which was not only difficult from a technical standpoint, it was also no picnic for several members of the film crew who suffered from a fear of heights.

For Jack and Jennifer's much anticipated wedding, *Days* took the crew to nearby Universal Studios for a Wild West–themed wedding, filled with many of the slapstick elements that had made the couple so popular. Two wedding dresses were made for Melissa Reeves, one designed to be used during many of the more outlandish stunts. In one such scene, Jack and Jennifer fell into a well. What the dress designers failed to take into consideration was that the dress would shrink after it dried. For all the subsequent stunts, Reeves had to wear the real wedding dress.

After Jason Brooks (PETER BLAKE) eloped with his girlfriend Corrine, his mother insisted on throwing him a wedding reception. The reception conflicted with a rooftop location shoot that *Days* had planned. Rather than ask his mother to reschedule the reception, Brooks—armed with a basket of cookies—went into the producers' office to ask them to reschedule the shoot.

The Line between Fact and Fiction

DOUG WILLIAMS AND JULIE OLSON were married in the same church where their portrayers, Bill Hayes and Susan Seaforth, had tied the knot just two years earlier. Instead of hiring an actor to portray the minister, the show hired the same minister who had married the Hayeses. The Hayeses also repeated some of the same vows they had recited during their real-life wedding.

When Kristian Alfonso (HOPE WILLIAMS BRADY) married British businessman Simon McCauley, she wore the same wedding dress that Hope had worn two years previously when Hope married Bo Brady. At first, Alfonso was only going to wear Hope's headpiece, but her husband-to-be convinced her to wear the whole thing. Unfortunately that old superstition about the groom not seeing the bride in her dress before the wedding turned out to be true. The Alfonso/McCauley union ended in divorce several years later.

One of Lane Davies's storylines as Dr. Evan Whyland involved artificial insemination. Because of Mickey Horton's sterility, his wife Maggie entered a surrogate motherhood program and learned that she was carrying Dr. Evan Whyland's daughter. (Years later, she discovered that Neil Curtis was the actual father.) When Davies moved on to the soap opera *Santa Barbara,* he was involved in a similar storyline. His character, Mason Capwell, was recruited by fellow lawyer Julia Wainwright to father a

While Doug Williams and Julie Olson were not the first popular couple on *Days*, their real-life romance added a dimension to their onscreen romance that transformed them into the show's supercouple for most of the 1970s. Luckily for Bill Hayes and Susan Seaforth Hayes, who have played Doug and Julie off and on for twenty-five years and counting, their real-life romance has run much more smoothly than that of their onscreen counterparts.

1. Doug Williams first learned of Salem while sharing a prison cell with which member of the Horton clan?

   (a) Dr. Tom Horton   (b) Bill Horton

   (c) Mickey Horton   (d) Mike Horton

2. Who paid Doug to romance Julie away from her husband Scott Banning?

   (a) Julie's mother, Addie   (b) Julie's mother-in-law

   (c) Scott's ex-wife   (d) Julie's romantic rival, Susan Hunter

3. What was the name of the cabaret where Doug first landed a singing job in Salem?

   (a) Wings (b) Blondie's (c) Sergio's (d) The Salem Lodge

4. What did Doug and Julie fight about that prompted him to elope with her mother Addie?

   (a) Julie insisted Doug give up his singing career for a better paying job.

   (b) Julie refused to take Doug's last name.

   (c) Doug objected to Julie's insistence that she bring her stepson David along with them on their honeymoon.

   (d) Julie refused to believe that Doug had not slept with Susan Hunter.

5. How was Addie killed?

    (a) She was shot by a burglar.

    (b) She was accidentally shot by Julie, who mistook her for a burglar.

    (c) She was hit by a car.

    (d) She was murdered by the Salem Strangler.

6. Doug's ex-wife Kim, a Polynesian princess, delayed his wedding to Julie by making what untrue claim against him?

    (a) She claimed that they were still married.

    (b) She accused him of murdering her father.

    (c) She claimed that he had murdered three of his wives.

    (d) She accused him of stealing all her money after marrying her.

7. In what country did Julie and Doug honeymoon after they finally got married?

    (a) France   (b) Italy   (c) Spain   (d) Egypt

8. How was Julie's face so badly scarred that she divorced Doug?

    (a) Susan Hunter threw acid in her face.

    (b) An oven exploded in her face.

    (c) She was pushed through a sliding glass door.

    (d) She was mauled by a grizzly bear while camping.

9. What is Doug and Julie's theme song?

    (a) "Love Is a Many Splendored Thing"

    (b) "Love Me Tender"

    (c) "Friends and Lovers"

    (d) "The Look of Love"

10. How many times have Doug and Julie been married?

    (a) once   (b) twice   (c) three times   (d) never legally

child for her. After playing out both of those stories, Davies was approached about donating a non-monetary contribution to an organization of single women who wished to become mothers.

In the early 1980s, as daytime was discovering its fascination with science fiction, *Days* introduced a robot onto the show. In the storyline, the robot named SICO was supposed to be used as a focusing point for children suffering from learning disabilities. The robot actually wound up reaching one troubled child in the audience in a very special way. Danny Smith, an autistic six-year-old, used to watch *Days* with his mother. Although he had never before laughed at anything he'd seen on television, a comic scene between the robot and Eugene Bradford (John de Lancie) made him laugh. His family and doctors built on that breakthrough, and he was eventually enrolled in a special school.

In the mid-1980s, Suzanne Rogers (MAGGIE HORTON) left the show after being diagnosed with myasthenia gravis, a life-threatening neuromuscular disease that caused her to become depressed and fatigued. When she returned to the show the following year, she requested that the producers write her illness into Maggie's storyline.

Macdonald Carey, who'd written several books of poetry, was given the chance to share some of his poems with the audience. Under the pseudonym Norm de Plume, Dr. Tom Horton recited his poetry at a local coffeehouse.

Antony Alda taped a scene in which his character, Johnny Corelli, was fired. As Alda was walking off the soundstage, producer Al Rabin walked up to tell him that the show was letting him go.

While out dining, Roberta Leighton (GINGER DAWSON), who played a doctor on *The Young and the Restless,* saved a fellow diner's life by performing CPR until the paramedics arrived.

Shortly after Deidre Hall went public about her efforts to have a child through surrogate motherhood, her character Marlena discussed the matter of infertility with her brother-in-law, Bo Brady. Bo had come to

Marlena to talk about his fiancée Carly Manning's infertility. The lines hit close to home for Hall as Marlena suggested to Bo that he could consider adoption—an option that Hall herself had considered over the years. The writers had wanted Marlena to suggest that Bo and Carly could find a surrogate mother when the time came, but Hall objected. Because her own use of a surrogate had garnered so much press, Hall felt the suggestion would steal the audience's attention away from the moment between Marlena and Bo and redirect it to her own private life.

Deidre Hall with her sons, Tully Chapin (in arms) and David Atticus (dressed as Dracula).

Naming Names

ALTHOUGH SPELLED DIFFERENTLY, the character of Marlena Evans was indirectly named after film legend Marlene Dietrich. During a technicians' strike back in 1976, Marlene Asher (who was named directly after Dietrich), was temporarily reassigned from her position as manager of finance and revenue for KNBC-TV in Los Angeles to manning the phones at *Days of Our Lives*. One of the directors Asher spoke with a number of times was taken with both her name and her voice. She turned him down when he asked her out but suggested that if he liked the name that much, he give it to a character on the show. Three months later, the character of psychiatrist Marlena Evans was introduced.

In the original bible for the show, the Hortons' presumed dead son Tommy was named Danny.

As revealed during the Satanic possession storyline, the town of Salem derived its name from "Shalom," the Hebrew word for peace.

Don Frabotta's character, Dave the maître d', spent seventeen years on *Days* without ever being given a last name.

Edward Mallory had gotten so accustomed to being called Bill Horton for the majority of his day that once when he was paged in an airport by his real name, he didn't respond.

When the character of Nick Corelli, the pimp, was first introduced on the show, he went by the last name Bartelli.

Scott Reeves played a teenaged troublemaker by the name of Jake Hogansen, an obvious play on the name of the show's leading man, Drake Hogestyn.

Since the character of Patch was conceived as a short-term villain, the simple nickname seemed to suffice. As the role expanded and members of Patch's family were added to the canvas, the writers realized that they needed to come up with a full name for the character. In tribute to the work of Stephen Nichols, who fleshed the role out into one of the better characters of the 1980s, the writers named Patch Steve. *General Hospital* also named the character Nichols plays on that show after the actor, with a slight variation—Stefan.

Stephen Nichols, though, was far from the first soap actor to have his character named after him. Robert Clary, who joined the show in 1972, not only played a character with the same first name but a last name nearly identical to his own: LeClair.

The character of Ivan Marais was originally named Pierre. As it turned out, Ivan G'Vera had a hard time remembering the name Pierre when he first began on the show. After G'Vera forgot his character's name during the second take of a scene, the director renamed the character Ivan. "Maybe now you'll remember it," the director said.

Due in strong part to the popularity of the romance between Patch and Kayla, Kayla became one of the most popular names for baby girls born in the late 1980s.

When the character of Jennifer Horton Deveraux was pregnant, viewers were given the chance to call in and vote on prospective baby names. They picked Abigail if it was a girl, which it was.

Billie Reed's middle name is Holliday. Like the character of Billie, the legendary jazz singer Billie Holliday suffered from an addiction to heroin.

On his first day of work, J. Eddie Peck walked into the producers' office to make some suggestions about his role. Although he had been hired to

Kristian Alfonso didn't want Hope's new love interest to share the same name as her son Gino, pictured here.

play a preppy con man by the name of Trey Hawkins, he told the producers that he didn't feel like someone named Trey. The producers came up with the name Hawk as a shortened form of the character's last name and asked him how he felt about that. Since he liked it better than Trey, he kept it. Along with the name change, the character was revamped from a preppy Easterner into more of a cowboy type.

When the role of Franco Kelly was originally created, the character was to be named Sean Kelly. It wasn't until Victor Alfieri auditioned for the part that the producers decided to give the character an Italian first name. Next, they planned to call the model/gigolo Gino Kelly. Kristian Alfonso, whose character Hope Williams would become somewhat romantically involved with Alfieri's character, objected to the name. Her son was named Gino, and she didn't want to be doing love scenes opposite a character with the same name as her son. With regard to the name Gino, it should be noted that Hope has several times believed that she might be a young woman named Gina, a feminized version of Gino.

Aremid, the mysterious town where Tony DiMera committed suicide and framed John Black for murder, is DiMera spelled backwards.

The foreign country from which Lawrence Alamain hails was never mentioned by name.

AKA

1. Which Horton read poetry in a coffee house under the nom de plume Norm de Plume?
(a) Tom   (b) Mickey   (c) Mike   (d) Alice

2. When Mickey Horton was suffering from amnesia and living on Maggie's farm, what name did he go by?
(a) Marty Hansen   (b) Ham McDonald
(c) Jack Smith   (d) Jack Farmer

3. What is Doug Williams's real name?

(a) William Douglas   (b) Brent Douglas

(c) Mark Brooks   (d) William Banning

4. When Brooke Hamilton returned from the presumed dead, what name did she use?

(a) Renée Francouer   (b) Kelly James

(c) Constance Gill   (d) Stephanie Woodruff

5. What name did Jessica Blake's promiscuous alternate personality call herself?

(a) Angel   (b) Barbie   (c) Christy   (d) Desirée

6. By what Shakespearean code name was Shane Donovan's brother Drew better known?

(a) Hamlet   (b) Romeo   (c) Iago   (d) Othello

7. What character was born with the name Billy Johnson?

(a) Jack Deveraux   (b) Justin Kiriakis

(c) Lucas Roberts   (d) Austin Reed

8. When Frankie Brady returned to Salem, it was revealed that he was Dr. Carly Manning's brother. What was their true family name?

(a) Van DerKellen   (b) Von Leuschner   (c) DeVilbus   (d) DeVilliers

9. What name did Stefano DiMera go by during his long-ago affair with Vivian Alamain?

(a) Francisco   (b) Sergio   (c) Rudolpho   (c) Guillermo

10. What is Celeste's real first name?

(a) Annie   (b) Betty   (c) Claire   (d) Frankie

The Names Have Been Changed

WHEN SUZANNE ROGERS (MAGGIE HORTON) was dancing with the Rockettes at Radio City Music Hall, she was still going by her given name, Suzanne Crumpler. Among the pieces of career advice she received along the way was a producer's suggestion that she change her name. Since she was a dancer and wanted to become an actress, her mother suggested that she pick Rogers in honor of Ginger Rogers, one of the most famous actress-dancers in film history.

It was probably not surprising to Robert Kelker-Kelly (BO BRADY) that there was already a Bobby Kelly in the actors union when he joined. He solved the problem by adding in his mother's family name, Kelker. From an emotional standpoint, Kelker-Kelly had wanted to distance himself somewhat from his father's last name since his father had walked out on the family when Kelker-Kelly was a boy.

After marrying former castmate Scott Reeves (JAKE HOGANSEN), Melissa Brennan (JENNIFER HORTON) took his last name to become Melissa Reeves.

When Susan Seaforth (JULIE OLSON) married her leading man Bill Hayes (DOUG WILLIAMS) she added his name to her own. She had been born Susan Seabold.

Tracey E. Bregman's (DONNA TEMPLE CRAIG) name has changed a bit over the years. She started out being billed as Tracey Bregman but added her middle initial upon the advice of a numerologist. When she married real estate developer Ron Recht, she became Tracey Bregman Recht. (She once joked that she didn't want to be known as Tracey E. Recht.) During a troubled period in her marriage, she reverted back to being called Tracey E. Bregman. Although she and her husband have reconciled their differences and remain married, she continues to go by the name Tracey E. Bregman.

When Hunter Tylo showed up on *Days* as Marina Toscano, many fans didn't recognize the brunette as Deborah Moorehart, the blonde actress who had played Robin McCall on *All My Children* just two years previously. The name change and the new hair color were outward signs of the changes Tylo was making in her own life. The last name Tylo she took after marrying fellow soap actor Michael Tylo; Hunter was her maiden name.

Like Hunter Tylo, Ariana Chase, who replaced Patsy Pease as Kimberly Brady, decided to rechristen herself as a symbol of the sense of rebirth she was feeling. She considered changing her first name as well, but realized that it was too intrinsic to her identity to lose. During the 1970s, Chase worked on a number of soap operas, including *As the World Turns,* under the name Ariana Munker, which itself started out as Muenker.

Cheryl-Ann Wilson (MEGAN HATHAWAY) was sporting the exotic new first name Miranda when she turned up as a psychic on *Santa Barbara.*

Louise Sorel (VIVIAN ALAMAIN) was born with the last name Cohen.

While it is not uncommon for actresses to take their husband's name, Wortham Krimmer (CAL WINTERS) has actually taken his wife's name. When Krimmer discovered that there was another Robert Krimmer in the actors union, he decided to expand his professional name to Robert Wortham Krimmer, adding his wife's maiden name to his own out of respect for the support that she'd given his acting career. When someone pointed out to him that, from a practical standpoint, his name was too long, he dropped his first name Robert and went by Wortham Krimmer. Friends, however, still call him Bob.

While most actors change their names to sound less ethnic, George Jenesky (NICK CORELLI), who was born with the WASP-ish moniker Conrad Dunn, took the opposite route. Since leaving *Days,* he has gone back to using his real name.

After producers refused to even see Braden Matthews (TRAVIS) for *The Greg Louganis Story* because his given surname, Sucietto, sounded too ethnic, he decided to change it. He picked the last name Matthews after his son Matthew. He has another son named Braden, so his professional name is a combination of his sons' first names.

Michael Bays (JULIO RAMIREZ) has gone back to using his given name, Michael Constantino. George Deloy, who played the villainous Orpheus in the mid-1980s, has also gone back to his birth name, George Del Hoyo.

Paul Kersey (ALAN HARRIS) was born Paul Neumann. Although the last name was spelled differently than Paul Newman, the movie star, the actors union insisted that he find another moniker.

Kevin Spirtas (DR. CRAIG WESLEY) went by Kevin Blair, his middle name, when he played Tom Gallagher on the syndicated soap *Rituals* back in the mid-1980s. Since that time, he's been through half a dozen name changes before coming full circle to Kevin Spirtas.

Robert Clary (ROBERT LECLAIR) was born Robert Max Wideman.

After coming to America from Czechoslovakia, Ivan G'Vera (IVAN MARAIS) discovered that people were having a difficult time pronouncing his given last name Splichal. He came up with the unusual name G'Vera by contracting together the first names of his father George and mother Vera. The idea, he has admitted, came to him while he was drinking. His father was more confused than flattered when G'Vera explained what he had done.

Drake is actually Drake Hogestyn's (JOHN BLACK) middle name. He used it as his first name for the first time when he entered a talent search/essay contest sponsored by Columbia Pictures. His first name is Donald.

Like Hogestyn, Macdonald Carey was also known by his middle name. His given first name was Edward.

Happy Birth-Days

January

3   Shannon Sturges (MOLLY BRINKER)

4   Rick Hearst (SCOTT BANNING)

17   Jane Elliot (ANJELICA DEVERAUX)

22   Robert Mailhouse (BRIAN SCOFIELD)

26   Tracey Middendorf (CARRIE BRADY)

29   Matthew Ashford (JACK DEVERAUX)

February

9   Charles Shaughnessy (SHANE DONOVAN)

16   Michael Easton (TANNER SCOFIELD)

19   Stephen Nichols (STEVE "PATCH" JOHNSON)

25   Leann Hunley (ANNA DIMERA)

March

1   Jensen Ackles (ERIC BRADY)

1   Jed Allan (DON CRAIG)

1   Robert Clary (ROBERT LeCLAIR)

9   Lauren Koslow (KATE ROBERTS)

9   Jaime Lyn Bauer (DR. LAURA HORTON)

9	Joe Gallison (Dr. Neil Curtis)
13	Joseph Mascolo (Stefano DiMera)
13	Robert S. Woods (Paul Stewart)
14	Melissa Reeves (Jennifer Horton Deveraux)
20	Tanya Boyd (Celeste)
20	John de Lancie (Eugene Bradford)
26	Billy Warlock (Frankie Brady)

Jensen Ackles (ERIC BRADY) shares his birthday with two Days alumni.

Austin Peck's (Austin Reed) April 9th birthday makes him an Aries.

April

1	Ivan G'Vera (Ivan Marais)
5	Krista Allen-Moritt (Billie Reed)
9	Austin Peck (Austin Reed)
14	John Clarke (Mickey Horton)
20	Adam Caine (Edmund Crumb)

May

7	Peter Reckell (BO BRADY)
8	Julianne Morris (SWAMP GIRL)
10	Lisa Linde (ALI)
10	Jason Brooks (PETER BLAKE)
11	Roark Critchlow (DR. MIKE HORTON)
12	Quinn Redeker (ALEX MARSHALL)
16	Scott Reeves (JAKE HOGANSEN)
23	Staci Greason (ISABELLA TOSCANO BLACK)
25	Marie-Alise Recasner (LYNN BURKE)
26	Genie Francis (DIANA COLVILLE)

June

2	Maree Cheatham (MARIE HORTON)
6	Ariane Zuker (NICOLE WALKER)
14	Edward Mallory (DR. BILL HORTON)
15	Eileen Davidson (KRISTEN BLAKE, SUSAN BANKS, et al)
23	Roberta Leighton (GINGER DAWSON)
25	Michael Sabatino (LAWRENCE ALAMAIN)

July

1	Frank Parker (SHAWN BRADY)
3	Hunter Tylo (MARINA TOSCANO)
5	Patsy Pease (KIMBERLY BRADY)
9	Suzanne Rogers (MAGGIE HORTON)
11	Susan Seaforth Hayes (JULIE OLSON WILLIAMS)

12	Judi Evans Luciano (ADRIENNE JOHNSON KIRIAKIS)
16	Philece Sampler (RENÉE DUMONDE)
24	John Aniston (VICTOR KIRIAKIS)
29	Bryan Dattilo (LUCAS ROBERTS)
29	Kevin Spirtas (CRAIG WESLEY)
30	Victor Alfieri (FRANCO KELLY)
31	Susan Flannery (DR. LAURA HORTON)
31	Wally Kurth (JUSTIN KIRIAKIS)
31	Lane Davies (DR. EVAN WHYLAND)

August

4	Crystal Chappell (DR. CARLY MANNING)
6	Louise Sorel (VIVIAN ALAMAIN)
10	James Reynolds (ABE CARVER)
22	John Lupton (DR. TOMMY HORTON)

September

3	Shelley Taylor Morgan (ANJELICA DEVERAUX)
4	Collin O'Donnell (SHAWN-DOUGLAS BRADY)
5	Kristian Alfonso (HOPE WILLIAMS BRADY)
10	Cheryl-Ann Wilson (MEGAN HATHAWAY)
19	Alison Sweeney (SAMI BRADY)
22	Lynn Herring (LISANNE GARDNER)
23	Patty Weaver (TRISH CLAYTON)
25	Josh Taylor (CHRIS KOSITCHEK and ROMAN BRADY)
29	Drake Hogestyn (JOHN BLACK)

October

5   Peter Brown (GREG PETERS)

10   J. Eddie Peck (HAWK HAWKINS)

14   Arleen Sorkin (CALLIOPE JONES)

15   Renée Jones (LEXIE CARVER)

25   Lisa Trusel (MELISSA HORTON JANNINGS)

31   Deidre Hall (DR. MARLENA EVANS)

31   Andrea Hall-Lovell (SAMANTHA EVANS)

November

3   Peggy McCay (CAROLINE BRADY)

11   Denise Alexander (SUSAN HUNTER)

13   Daniel Pilon (GAVIN STONE)

23   David Wallace (TOD CHANDLER)

December

9   Frances Reid (ALICE HORTON)

10   Gloria Loring (LIZ CURTIS)

12   Holly Gagnier (IVY JANNINGS)

13   Christie Clark (CARRIE BRADY REED)

14   Elaine Princi (LINDA ANDERSON)

20   Karen Moncrieff (GABRIELLE PASCAL)

27   Barbara Crampton (TRISTA EVANS)

31   Don Diamont (CARLO FORENZA)

Facts about the Stars

the NAMING PROCESS

Macdonald Carey's (DR. TOM HORTON) aunt Marie was nicknamed Dool, the same nickname fans and soap magazines would years later give to *Days of Our Lives*.

Deidre Hall (DR. MARLENA EVANS) has long loved the name Atticus. Back in the 1970s, she owned a cat named Atticus, and more recently she gave it to her firstborn son David as a middle name.

The town of Ocilla, Georgia, honored Joseph Mascolo (STEFANO DIMERA) for his charitable work in the area by naming a street after him: Mascolo Drive.

A street in Georgia was named after Joseph Mascolo (STEFANO DIMERA).

Roark Critchlow (DR. MIKE HORTON) was named after Howard Roark, the lead character in the Ayn Rand novel, *The Fountainhead*, which his father had been reading about the same time that Critchlow was born. While growing up, however, Roark used the name Grant. Critchlow took his daughter's name Jara from a song by the Irish rock group U2. His other daughter is named Reign.

Mary Beth Evans (KAYLA BRADY) had considered naming her son after her former leading man Charles Shaughnessy, but ultimately decided on the name Matthew instead.

Leann Hunley (ANNA DiMERA) was named after former Miss America Lee Meriwether, who at the time went by the name Lee Ann.

In high school, Lisa Rinna's (BILLIE REED) gift for facial expressions earned her the nickname "Rubberface." The license plate on Rinna's parents' car reads *DOOL*.

The J in J. Eddie Peck (HAWK HAWKINS) stands for John, his father's name.

Thyme Lewis's (DR. JONAH CARVER) father, a jazz musician, came up with the name Thyme by combining the words "rhythm" and "time."

GROWING UP

There was no indoor plumbing on her grandmother's farm, where Renée Jones (LEXIE CARVER) spent the early years of her life. Among the inconveniences that entailed, she took her baths in an outside tub and drew water from the well. Jones lived on the farm with four siblings and eight cousins.

Thaao Penghlis (ANDRÉ DiMERA) was so poor growing up that he didn't even have a bed. He slept on the dining room table.

David Wallace (TOD CHANDLER) was such a rebellious teenager that his parents kicked him out of the house.

Shannon Tweed (SAVANNAH WILDER) moved out on her own at the age of fifteen.

Maree Cheatham's (MARIE HORTON) mother was married seven times before Cheatham turned twelve.

Growing up, Barbara Crampton (TRISTA EVANS) spent her summers traveling the carnival circuit with her father, who ran a basketball game.

Among Hunter Tylo's (MARINA TOSCANO) pets when she was growing up were three boa constrictors and an alligator.

At the age of sixteen, Victor Alfieri (FRANCO KELLY) shaved his head in homage to his movie idol Yul Brynner.

Since spending his summers working on a ranch owned by his grandfather, Wally Kurth (JUSTIN KIRIAKIS) has adopted a vegetarian diet.

RELIGION

Stephen Nichols (STEVE "PATCH" JOHNSON) once intended to become a monk.

Drake Hogestyn (JOHN BLACK) was the only member of his family not baptized.

Macdonald Carey (DR. TOM HORTON) met Pope John Paul II twice.

Patrick Muldoon (AUSTIN REED) served during Mass as an altar boy.

Because of his religious beliefs, Austin Peck (AUSTIN REED) has made a commitment to remaining celibate until he marries.

Brian L. Green (ALAN BRAND) is descended from a long line of ministers and preachers. Although he didn't follow in their footsteps as expected, he was once a singer for the PTL Club.

Julianne Morris's (SWAMP GIRL) parents were missionaries. She has done missionary work and plans to do more in the future, both domestically and internationally. She broke up with one boyfriend, talk show host Mike Berger of *Mike & Maty,* over their religious differences: he is Catholic, she is Protestant.

EDUCATION

Robert Kelker-Kelly (BO BRADY) was kicked out of high school after pushing the headmaster over a chair.

Renée Jones (LEXIE CARVER) graduated from high school by the time she was sixteen.

Steve Wilder (JACK DEVERAUX) graduated from high school at the age of fourteen.

Tracey E. Bregman (DONNA CRAIG) went to the Westlake School for Girls with the daughters of Carol Burnett and Raquel Welch.

Bryan Dattilo (LUCAS ROBERTS) graduated from Beverly Hills High School. Among other soap actors who were there at the same time was Steve Burton, who played Harris Michaels on *Days* and is best known as Jason Quartermaine Morgan on *General Hospital*.

Josh Taylor (CHRIS KOSITCHEK/ROMAN BRADY) earned a bachelor's degree in sociology from Dartmouth and a law degree from the University of Colorado.

John Aniston (VICTOR KIRIAKIS) has a bachelor of science degree in biology from California State University.

Drake Hogestyn (JOHN BLACK) majored in microbiology at the University of Southern Florida–Tampa.

Ivan G'Vera (IVAN MARAIS) has a degree in electrical engineering. He also graduated from the University of Michigan with a bachelor's degree in education.

Michael Easton (TANNER SCOFIELD) earned a bachelor of science degree from UCLA, majoring in history, particularly Greek history. He went to high school with Michael Brainard (JOEY MARTIN, *All My Children*; TED CAPWELL, *Santa Barbara*).

Richard Biggs, who played Dr. Marcus Hunter, once considered pursuing a career in medicine. He went to the University of Southern California with future *Days* castmate Michael T. Weiss (DR. MIKE HORTON).

Charles Shaughnessy (SHANE DONOVAN) studied law at Cambridge University in England.

Before playing father and son on *Days*, Joseph Mascolo (STEFANO DIMERA) and Thaao Penghlis (TONY DIMERA) met while taking the same acting class.

One of Eileen Davidson's (KRISTEN BLAKE/SUSAN BANKS, et al) first acting teachers was Peggy McCay (CAROLINE BRADY).

Bill Hayes's (DOUG WILLIAMS) fascination with his family tree led him to study genealogy at West Virginia University in his grandparents' hometown. He continued his studies toward a Ph.D. at UCLA and Cal State–Northridge.

Macdonald Carey (DR. TOM HORTON) donated his personal library containing over six hundred books to UCLA.

ODD JOBS

Matthew Ashford (JACK DEVERAUX) learned how to juggle practically overnight when he and a friend landed jobs as jugglers.

Charles Shaughnessy (SHANE DONOVAN) sold triple X-rated videos over the telephone and worked for a few days as a private investigator.

Judi Evans (ADRIENNE JOHNSON KIRIAKIS) was a circus clown at the age of two.

Robert Kelker-Kelly's (BO BRADY) jobs have ranged from bouncer to secretary for nine women in an office.

Mark Drexler (ROGER LOMBARD) worked as contractor and architect. Among his clients was former castmate Robert Kelker-Kelly.

At age eighteen, J. Eddie Peck (HAWK HAWKINS) worked as a disc jockey for a radio station.

Staci Greason (ISABELLA TOSCANO BLACK) worked in a publicity firm that handled such hit sitcoms as *Roseanne* and *The Cosby Show*.

In between her acting roles on *One Life to Live* and *Days of Our Lives,* Judith Chapman (ANJELICA DEVERAUX) developed film for a photographer.

Wally Kurth (JUSTIN KIRIAKIS) sold motel art by telephone.

Richard Biggs (DR. MARCUS HUNTER) dug ditches.

Crystal Chappell (DR. CARLY MANNING) wrote obituaries.

While in his teens, Braden Matthews (TRAVIS) worked as a junior zoologist caring for injured animals including crocodiles and monkeys.

Even after Shannon Sturges (MOLLY BRINKER) landed the role of Molly Brinker, she still kept her job as a personal assistant to an educational therapist, running errands to the bank and dry cleaners.

Roark Critchlow (DR. MIKE HORTON) has held down a variety of jobs from bartender to lumberjack to janitor. The aspect of janitoring he hated the most was picking cigarette butts out of the urinals.

MILITARY TRAINING

Mark Valley (JACK DEVERAUX) graduated from West Point. As an Army combat engineer and lieutenant, Valley was put in charge of explosives and demolition.

While working for the Information Service Office, James Reynolds (ABE CARVER) wrote for the service newspaper, *The Windward Marine*. As part of his duties, he was sent to Vietnam to report on various battles. There he was wounded.

John Aniston (VICTOR KIRIAKIS) served in the U.S. Navy Intelligence as a lieutenant commander.

Robert S. Woods (PAUL STEWART) served with the Green Berets in Vietnam.

Peter Brown (GREG PETERS) started a theater group while stationed with the army in Alaska.

Victor Alfieri's (FRANCO KELLY) face was smashed during a mugging attempt in the streets of Rome where he grew up. His anger over the incident compelled him to join the police academy and become a police officer (which in Italy is a branch of the military) once his injuries had healed.

Braden Matthews (TRAVIS) suffered from post-traumatic stress syndrome after serving in Grenada and Beirut.

AT HOME

Jed Allan's (DON CRAIG) second home, Windy Gables, was owned by movie legend Clark Gable and his lover Carole Lombard. The silent film classic *The Son of the Sheik* was filmed there.

Jensen Ackles (ERIC BRADY) sleeps with a pink stuffed pig that he named Coke after spilling Coke all over him.

Richard Biggs (DR. MARCUS HUNTER) used to live out of his car, which he kept overnight in the parking lot of a gym.

In November of 1996, Peter Reckell's (BO BRADY) house burned to the ground.

CRIME AND PUNISHMENT

While in Florida, Bill Hayes (DOUG WILLIAMS) was once pulled over by a line of police cars and handcuffed. None of the officers would tell him what was going on. He soon discovered that he not only was driving the same make car as an armed killer but he fit the killer's physical description as well.

While walking around Los Angeles, a city where everyone drives, Victor Alfieri (FRANCO KELLY) has several times been mistaken for a male prostitute.

While Don Frabotta (DAVE, THE WAITER) was gardening in his own yard, a lunatic attacked him with a metal pipe. Because the pipe never made contact with Frabotta, the police let the attacker go.

Back in the late 1950s, Jay Robinson (MONTY DOLAN) was arrested for drug possession and sentenced to a California penitentiary.

James Reynolds (ABE CARVER) was pulled over for speeding but escaped with a warning because the police officer was a fan.

Billy Hufsey, who played a former gang member on *Days*, has worked to rehabilitate gang members in the Los Angeles area, sometimes using his character as an example of someone who turned himself around.

A burglar tried to break into Roberta Leighton's (GINGER DAWSON) apartment the same day that she was off filming an episode of the crime series *Barnaby Jones*.

One New Year's Eve, Staci Greason (ISABELLA TOSCANO BLACK) and her boyfriend were robbed at gunpoint. Because Greason did not see the gun, which was pressed into her boyfriend's chest, she hesitated handing over her purse, which contained only one dollar in cash. A week later, someone tried to steal her car out of the parking lot where she kept it.

For defecting to the United States, Ivan G'Vera (IVAN MARAIS) was sentenced *in absentia* by the Czechoslovakian government to a year in prison and was forbidden from returning to the country for ten years.

SPORTS

Kristian Alfonso (HOPE WILLIAMS BRADY) won a gold medal in figure skating at the Junior Olympics at the age of thirteen. A bobsledding accident cut short her plans to continue on to the Olympics.

After playing professional football with the Cleveland Browns and the Philadelphia Eagles, Matt Battaglia's (J. L. KING) career was tackled by a shoulder injury.

K. T. Stevens's (HELEN MARTIN) son Chris Marlowe captained the U.S. men's volleyball team, which won a gold medal at the 1984 Olympics.

Lorenzo Caccialanza (NICO) played professional soccer in Italy for more than a decade.

While at the University of California–Irvine, Michael Sabatino (LAWRENCE ALAMAIN) set a pole vaulting record of 17½ feet. He went on to train for the Olympics but came in thirteenth place in the 1976 Olympic trials.

Thaao Penghlis's (TONY DIMERA) record for the hundred-meter hurdle in Australia held for ten years.

Ivan G'Vera (IVAN MARAIS) coached soccer at Beverly Hills High School.

When he was still in high school, Drake Hogestyn (JOHN BLACK) was approached by the St. Louis Cardinals baseball team. He turned down their offer, opting instead to attend college. After graduating from college, he played third base for the New York Yankees farm team. An injury curtailed his career and kept him from ever advancing to the majors.

An injury curtailed Drake Hogestyn's (JOHN BLACK) plans to play in the major leagues.

Hobbies

Frances Reid (ALICE HORTON) has traveled to South America with the archaeology department from UCLA and to Sumatra and Jakarta with a team from the Smithsonian Institute.

Austin Peck (AUSTIN REED) collects comic books and would like to create his own comic one day.

Like his replacement, Patrick Muldoon collects comic books as well as baseball cards.

Louise Sorel (VIVIAN ALAMAIN) collects three-foot-tall marionettes.

Jeff Griggs (JUDE ST. CLAIR) practices magic and has wrestled himself out of more than one straightjacket. His hobby nearly cost him his life on one occasion when he almost drowned in a water tank.

Robert Mailhouse (BRIAN SCOFIELD) collects motorcycles.

An avid potter, Maree Cheatham (MARIE HORTON) has had showings of her work.

Patrick Muldoon (AUSTIN REED) does imitations of Mick Jagger, Robert DeNiro, Al Pacino (in *Scarface*), and several of his former castmates: Jason Brooks, Drake Hogestyn, Robert Kelker-Kelly, and Lisa Rinna.

While camping in the woods, Michael Sabatino (LAWRENCE ALAMAIN) has stared down more than one bear.

James Reynolds (ABE CARVER) collects old radios as well as tapes of old radio shows.

Celebrity Encounters

In all her shows on Broadway, Louise Sorel (VIVIAN ALAMAIN) was never drawn by Al Hirschfeld, most famous for his caricatures in the Arts & Leisure section of the Sunday *New York Times*. After running into him twice during a 1996 trip to New York, Sorel, who owns three originals of his work (including a self-portrait), took matters into her own hands and commissioned him to do a caricature of her.

Screen legend Katharine Hepburn once painted a portrait of Jay Robinson (MONTY DOLAN).

Richard Burgi (PHILIP COLLIER) was once stuck in an elevator with Katharine Hepburn.

A great admirer of architecture, Joseph Mascolo (STEFANO DIMERA) was thrilled to meet and get an autograph from famed architect Frank Lloyd Wright in New York City's Guggenheim Museum.

While waiting tables in New York, Crystal Chappell (DR. CARLY MANNING) served Oscar winner F. Murray Abraham (*Amadeus*) and got into a discussion on acting with him.

Among the celebrities in the aerobics class Holly Gagnier (IVY SELEJKO JANNINGS) taught at Jane Fonda's workout center were Sally Field and Lesley Ann Warren.

Kenny Jezek (LARS ENGLUND) danced onstage with Diana Ross at the 1986 American Music Awards.

Following in the footsteps of his father, stuntman Dick Warlock, Billy Warlock (FRANKIE BRADY) became a stuntman shortly after graduating from high school. Among his jobs was working as a stunt double for Robin Williams on the sitcom *Mork and Mindy*.

While writing for the *Topeka Daily Capitol*, James Reynolds (ABE CARVER) interviewed such stars as Jack Nicholson, Michael Douglas, and Peter Fonda.

When he was twelve years old, Bryan Dattilo saw *Dirty Harry* star Clint Eastwood leaving a restaurant. He walked up to the actor and said, "Go ahead, make my day." Rather than wait for a response, Dattilo ran away.

Jensen Ackles (ERIC BRADY) has hung around at *The Tonight Show*, which tapes right next door to *Days,* in order to meet the guests. Among the celebrities he has made a point to meet are basketball great Michael Jordan and country superstar Garth Brooks.

Beauty Contests

At the age of twelve, Deidre Hall (Dr. Marlena Evans) was named Junior Orange Bowl Queen.

Krista Allen-Moritt (Billie Reed) won a number of local beauty pageants in her hometown of Houston, and was once named the "Texas Budweiser girl" in a national advertising campaign, which placed her face everywhere from billboards to magazines and calendars.

Jaime Lyn Bauer (Dr. Laura Horton) was named Junior Miss Phoenix Crown and made it into the finals of the Miss Arizona pageant. After moving to Chicago, she was named Miss Chicago and was second runner-up for the title of Miss Illinois.

Karen Moncrieff (Gabrielle Pascal) was named Miss Illinois and competed in the Miss America pageant.

Charlotte Ross, who played Moncrieff's onscreen daughter Eve Donovan, represented Illinois in the Dreamgirl USA pageant, which brought her to the attention of composer-producer Giorgio Moroder.

In high school, Christie Clark (Carrie Brady) was named Freshman Princess. Queen of the Court that year was Janet Evans, who has won three Olympic gold medals for swimming.

Hunter Tylo (Marina Toscano) was once named Miss Fort Worth.

Deke Anderson, who played the villainous Eddie, has been named Mr. Nevada on several occasions and has gone on to emcee bodybuilding competitions.

Game Shows

From 1971 to '78, Jed Allan pulled double duty, playing Don Craig and hosting *Celebrity Bowling*, in which pairs of stars bowled against each other to win money for the studio audience. When the show was revived briefly in the late 1980s as *The New Celebrity Bowling*, Allan hosted again.

Bryan Dattilo (LUCAS ROBERTS) got his then girlfriend's permission to appear on MTV's dating game show *Singled Out*.

Alison Sweeney (SAMI BRADY) has been set up on dates on both *Singled Out* and on the syndicated *The Dating Game*.

Lorenzo Caccialanza (NICO) competed on an Italian version of *The Dating Game*, whose title translates to *She Loves Me, She Loves Me Not*. His two-year affair with the show's married hostess became a national scandal.

Bill Hayes and Susan Seaforth Hayes (DOUG and JULIE WILLIAMS) participated in a special costumed week on *The Hollywood Squares* dressed up as Adam and Eve.

Wally Kurth won twelve thousand dollars, a roll-top desk, and a set of encyclopedias competing on the *Hollywood Squares*-inspired game show *All Star Blitz*. After the show, host Peter Marshall told Kurth, "I think you're going to go far."

POSING FOR *PLAYBOY*

Shannon Tweed (SAVANNAH WILDER) not only posed for *Playboy*, she was the 1982 Playmate of the Year and dated *Playboy* founder Hugh Hefner as well.

A six-months pregnant Lisa Rinna (BILLIE REED) did a 1998 pictorial that included full frontal nudity.

While in the midst of making horror films, Barbara Crampton (TRISTA EVANS) posed topless in a horror movie-themed pictorial.

A 1982 pictorial involving the women of daytime television included Roberta Leighton (GINGER DAWSON) and Jaime Lyn Bauer (DR. LAURA HORTON), both of whom were working on *The Young and the Restless* at the time. Leighton wore a see-through teddy while Bauer posed completely nude. Ironically, there was a quote from Bauer in the piece saying that she would prefer not to be doing so many sex scenes on her show. Bauer has subsequently turned down roles that require any degree of nudity.

Holly Gagnier (Ivy Selejko Jannings) turned down the opportunity to be the *Playboy* centerfold as well as a number of movies that required nudity.

Psychic Phenomena

A psychic in Australia predicted that Thaao Penghlis (Tony DiMera) would become a successful actor. After Penghlis landed his role on *Days*, he tried to find the psychic without success. Someone who had read about Penghlis and the psychic in a soap magazine contacted the actor with the psychic's whereabouts. As it turned out, the psychic, like Penghlis, had emigrated to the United States. When Penghlis finally got in contact with the man, he learned that the psychic's wife and daughter were fans of the show.

When Jane Windsor (Emma Donovan) was twelve, her grandfather, a gypsy, told her, "You shall be seen in a great glass and live your life through that of another." It wasn't until she landed her role on *Days* that she understood that the great glass her grandfather referred to was a television set and that living her life through that of another referred to acting.

Crystal Chappell's (Dr. Carly Manning) grandmother was a longtime *Days* fan. One time, when Chappell was in the room with her while it was on, her grandmother told her, "You're going to be on that soap one day."

Tanya Boyd (Celeste) has had several out-of-body experiences.

Braden Matthews (Travis) believes that he was a frontiersman and a Native American in previous lives.

One apartment that Jaime Lyn Bauer (Dr. Laura Horton) lived in was haunted. In addition to plants inexplicably dying and the cat reacting to something no one else could see, Bauer herself once ran into an invisible wall in her bedroom.

Unscripted Kisses

DURING THE EARLY 1970s, Bill Hayes and Susan Seaforth became the first couple of daytime television. Not only were Doug and Julie the most popular couple during one of *Days'* most popular periods, Hayes and Seaforth had become an item backstage as well. For their first date, Hayes asked Seaforth out for a glass of champagne after work. When the time came to propose marriage, Hayes paid a visit to Seaforth's mother, actress-writer Elizabeth Harrower. He showed up at her door in a costume from *Oklahoma*, a play he was working in. When he asked Harrower for her daughter's hand in marriage, Harrower joked, "You'll have to take *all* of her." So Hayes did. Hayes and Seaforth married in 1974, two years before their onscreen counterparts made it to the altar. The Hayeses honeymooned in Italy just as Doug and Julie would. And while Doug and Julie have been married three times, the Hayeses have remained together consistently for the past twenty-three years, making theirs not only one of daytime's but also one of Hollywood's most successful marriages.

One of the greatest backstage romances was the one between Ted Corday, who co-created *Days of Our Lives,* and its longtime executive producer Betty Corday. The two met while working on a production of the Broadway play *John Henry;* Ted was directing it, Betty (then Betty Shay) was working as a production assistant. They went on to work as directors on a number of radio soaps—Betty on *Pepper Young's Family* and *Young Dr. Malone;* Ted on *The Woman in White* and *The Guiding Light.* When Ted died in 1966, Betty assumed the role of executive producer, a position

During the 1970s, Bill Hayes and Susan Seaforth Hayes (DOUG and JULIE WILLIAMS) were the First Couple of Daytime Television.

she shared over the years with, among others, Wes Kenney. Occasionally she listed herself as Mrs. Ted Corday on the Emmy ballots.

Although their time on *Days* barely overlapped, Denise Alexander (Susan Hunter) fell in love with and many years later married Richard Colla, who originated the role of Tony Merritt. The two have worked behind the scenes together, forming their own production company.

Although Alex Marshall and Dr. Marlena Evans cared little for each other onscreen, their portrayers, Quinn Redeker and Deidre Hall, were a backstage couple for several years. Hall was reputed to have gotten jealous watching Redeker do love scenes with other actresses. Hall is currently married to novelist Steve Sohmer, author of *Favorite Son*, and was once romantically linked to *General Hospital* alumnus/*MacGyver* star Richard Dean Anderson.

Gloria Loring, who had once been married to actor/talk show host Alan Thicke (*Growing Pains*), fell in love with Don Diamont, whose character Carlo Forenza had been introduced to cause trouble between Loring's character Liz and her husband Neil. Despite a sixteen-year age difference and Loring's initial impression that Diamont was cocky, the two found themselves drawn to each other. While the fans reacted badly to their onscreen love story, they rooted for Diamont and Loring as a real-life couple. Their backstage romance, however, ended after Diamont left the show.

Diamont joined the cast of *The Young and the Restless*, where he became involved with one of the show's leading ladies, Eileen Davidson, who at the time was playing Ashley Abbott. Diamont's character, Brad Carlton, was involved with Ashley's sister Traci. Like Loring, Davidson did not care too much for Diamont the first time she met him. It wasn't until after she left the show that the two began dating.

Davidson, who has been linked with a number of actors, among them Oscar winner Jon Voight, is currently married to Jon Lindstrom, who, like herself, has played multiple roles on his shows *General Hospital* and its spin-off *Port Charles*. He's played mentally unstable twins while Davidson has played eccentric quadruplets.

Lindstrom's current leading lady on *Port Charles*, Lynn Herring, has been married since the early 1980s to one of *Days'* more popular actors, Wayne Northrop (ROMAN BRADY). Northrop met Herring while the two were taking an acting class together. Shortly after Northrop returned to *Days* in the early '90s, Herring left *General Hospital* to take on the role of the scheming lawyer Lisanne Gardner on *Days*. In one of the few scenes they shared together, Roman, disguised as a housekeeper, dumped a vacuum bag on Lisanne's head. After Lisanne was killed off, Herring headed back to *General Hospital*. She and Northrop worked together most recently on *Port Charles*, where their characters were briefly married.

While playing Dr. Casey Reed on *The Young and the Restless*, Roberta Leighton (GINGER DAWSON) had an on again/off again relationship with castmate David Hasselhoff (*Baywatch*). All too much like an onscreen soap couple, the two were engaged three times but never made it to the altar. After leaving *Y&R* for *General Hospital*, Leighton got involved with that show's star Tony Geary. But it was another *General Hospital* actor whom she ended up marrying: Corey Young, who played Dr. Walt Benson after Leighton had returned to *Y&R*. The two met through their mutual publicist, who asked Young to accompany Leighton to a charity benefit. Young, it should be noted, was one of the many actors over the years considered for the frequently recast role of Jack Deveraux.

Both Lauren Koslow (KATE ROBERTS) and Jaime Lyn Bauer (DR. LAURA HORTON) met their husbands while working on the soap opera *The Young and the Restless*. Koslow's husband Nick Schillace and Bauer's husband Jeremy Swan both worked as makeup artists on the show. Koslow was a little intimidated by Schillace at first and never wanted to sit in his chair. Bauer and Swan kept their relationship very quiet because the producers didn't like the idea of employees fraternizing with one another.

Karen Kelly, who played Brenda Clegg on *Capitol* in the mid-1980s, was immediately taken with Ken Jezek (LARS ENGLUND) the first time she saw him on *Days of Our Lives*. A couple of weeks later, the two ran into each other at the opening of a restaurant. Jezek, who had recently separated from his wife, later called Kelly at her show to ask her out.

Billy Warlock (FRANKIE BRADY) was introduced to Marcy Walker (EDEN CAPWELL, *Santa Barbara*) by one of the producers on her show. At first, Walker doubted that Warlock liked her, but she took the bull by the horns, found out his number, and called him up. The two married and divorced two years later, three weeks after they had bought a house together. While filming a movie of the week, Walker fell in love with another man and ended the marriage with a telephone call. (His engagement to his *Baywatch* costar Erika Eleniak would end in a painfully similar fashion; just after setting a wedding date, she would call him from location to tell him that she had met someone new.) Warlock once said that Billy's onscreen breakup with Jennifer Horton (Melissa Reeves) helped him come to terms with his and Walker's divorce.

Among the varied daytime actresses movie star Alec Baldwin dated prior to marrying Kim Basinger was Holly Gagnier (IVY SELEJKO JANNINGS). The two met while Baldwin was playing a wife-abusing preacher on the primetime soap opera *Knots Landing*. Gagnier had dropped by the set to visit her father, Hugh, who was a director of photography for the show.

While making films in Europe, Louise Sorel (VIVIAN ALAMAIN) was pursued by such foreign film stars as Oliver Reed and Maurice Chevalier. While she dodged their romantic advances, she has married two actors: the late Herb Edelman, best known for his recurring role as Bea Arthur's ex-husband on *The Golden Girls*, and Ken Howard, best known for his starring role in the CBS high school basketball drama *The White Shadow*.

Crystal Chappell and Michael Sabatino met and fell in love while playing former lovers Dr. Carly Manning and Lawrence Alamain. The two went public about their romance during a fan club luncheon in 1991. A fan asked if they were dating in real life, and they admitted that they were. Although Carly had been paired in a popular romance with leading man Bo Brady, the backstage romance started seeping into the onscreen storyline as Carly rediscovered feelings for Lawrence. The actors were written off the show together and ended up eventually on East Coast ABC soaps: Chappell as a cigarette-smoking nun on *One Life to Live* and Sabatino as a pill pushing doctor on *All My Children*. While living in New York the two tied the knot at City Hall.

Scott Reeves was not on *Days of Our Lives* for very long—he had a small role as tough kid Jake in the teen storyline in 1988—but long enough for him to meet his future wife, Melissa Brennan (JENNIFER HORTON). Costar Michael Bays (JULIO RAMIREZ) helped bring them together. Their first official date was the party celebrating *Days'* twenty-fourth anniversary. After a couple of months dating, Reeves proposed on April Fool's Day.

Among Melissa Brennan's other boyfriends have been Ricky Paull Goldin (DEAN FRAME, *Another World*), who once described her as his "first love," and Jon Hensley (HOLDEN SNYDER, *As the World Turns*). Brennan and Hensley met at a personal appearance and dated bicoastally until Hensley left his show to move West and in with Brennan for eight months.

Both Goldin and Hensley have also dated other actresses from *Days of Our Lives*. When Hunter Tylo was living in New York and working on *All My Children,* she went out with Hensley. And in the early 1990s, Goldin dated Charlotte Ross (EVE DONOVAN). After three months together, they broke up while in New York together for the Daytime Emmy Awards.

Marie-Alise Recasner (NURSE LYNN) briefly dated Sean Penn while they were taking acting classes together.

While working on the horror series *Nightmare Café*, Jack Coleman (JAKE KOSITCHEK) met Beth Toussant, who has worked on such soaps as *Dallas* and *Savannah*. They married in 1996.

While working together on the primetime serial *Bare Essence*, Genie Francis (DIANA COLVILLE) met her future husband, *Star Trek: The Next Generation*'s Jonathan Frakes, who had a small role on *Days* in the mid-1980s as Jared McCallister. After *Bare Essence*, Frakes and Francis landed roles on the mini-series *North and South*. Francis never popped up on *Star Trek*, but the two played husband and wife in the big screen comedy *Camp Nowhere* and on the television series *Lois & Clark: The New Adventures of Superman*.

Despite a ten-year difference in their ages, David Wallace (TOD CHANDLER) found himself very attracted to Lisa Trusel (MELISSA HORTON JANNINGS) almost from the moment he joined the cast. During a public appearance in Toronto, the two of them shared a kiss. Trusel, who was dating someone at the time, promised to break up with her boyfriend as soon as she got back to Los Angeles. Two months later, Wallace and Trusel became engaged. Wallace believed that the producers were none too thrilled with their romance. He once told *Soap Opera Digest* he suspected that his relationship with Trusel cost him his job. When Wallace and Trusel finally tied the knot, his onscreen sister Gloria Loring (LIZ CURTIS) sang at the wedding.

The age difference between Robert Kelker-Kelly (BO BRADY) and Miriam Parrish was even greater than that between David Wallace and Lisa Trusel. Parrish was in her mid-teens when she joined the cast as Jamie Caldwell. Kelker-Kelly, at the time, was in his early thirties. The couple grew close while he helped her with her English homework. Because of the age difference, Kelker-Kelly made a conscious decision to back away from the relationship that was developing between them. Ironically, Parrish once told *Soap Opera Digest*: "It's fun working with gorgeous male actors, but I'm jail bait. That pretty much sums it up." As soon as Parrish turned eighteen, however, the two went public with their romance. After Kelker-Kelly and Parrish left the show, the two were married. Prior to Parrish, Kelker-Kelly had been married to a production assistant on *Another World*, whom he met while playing Sam Fowler on the show.

Peter Reckell (BO BRADY) met his current wife, Kelly Moneymaker, while making a personal appearance in Wyoming; she was there singing backup for Connie Stevens. Reckell met his first wife, Dale Kristien, when she played Victor's maid Janet on *Days*. Prior to Reckell, Kristien had been

Peter Reckell met his first wife,
Dale Kristien, on the show.

married to Sam Behrens (JAKE MYERS, *General Hospital*; GREGORY RICHARDSON, *Sunset Beach*).

Former Playmate Shannon Tweed (SAVANNAH WILDER) has dated *Playboy* founder Hugh Hefner himself and has been involved for more than a decade with Gene Simmons, bassist for the rock group Kiss. The two met at a party given at the Playboy mansion.

Lorenzo Caccialanza (NICO) dated Oscar winner Jane Fonda, who dumped him for media mogul Ted Turner.

Edward Mallory's character, Bill Horton, spent many of his years on the show chasing after his brother Mickey's wife, Laura. Behind the scenes, Mallory fell in love with his onscreen daughter-in-law, Suzanne Zenor, who played Mike's wife, Margo. They have been married for many years now. Prior to Zenor, Mallory had been married to Joyce Bulifant, best known for playing Gavin MacLeod's wife on *The Mary Tyler Moore Show*.

Heather North, who played Sandy Horton from the late 1960s to early '70s, is married to former director-producer H. Wesley Kenney.

Susan Diol (EMMY BORDEN) is married to former Hardy Boy/pop singer-turned-producer Shaun Cassidy.

John Aniston (VICTOR KIRIAKIS) met his wife, Sherry Rooney, while working together on the now defunct soap opera *Love of Life*.

Lisa Rinna (BILLIE REED) met her husband Harry Hamlin through a mutual friend.

While it is not uncommon for actors to fall in love with their leading ladies, Rod Arrants, who played crooked police chief Richard Cates, was once married to Patricia Estrin, who played his sister on the soap *Lovers and Friends*.

Among the varied celebrities Billy Hufsey (EMILIO RAMIREZ) has dated are Kristian Alfonso (HOPE WILLIAMS BRADY), Jacklyn Zeman (BOBBIE SPENCER JONES, *General Hospital*) and *Wheel of Fortune*'s Vanna White.

Victor Alfieri and Kristian Alfonso (FRANCO KELLY and
HOPE BRADY) kept their fans and the press
guessing about their offscreen relationship.

Julianne Morris (Swamp Girl) started going out with Eddie Cibrian (Cole Deschanel, *Sunset Beach*) while they were working together on *The Young and the Restless*. Their onscreen romance took a decidedly unromantic turn when his character Matt raped her and she shot him. Their offscreen relationship stood out among the crop of young Hollywood romances because of Morris's public affirmation that she intended to remain celibate until she was legally wed. Morris has not described too many of the details about their breakup except to say that Cibrian was not as honest with her as she'd been with him.

Although Kristian Alfonso and Victor Alfieri (Hope and Franco) were seen together acting more than friendly with each other at several functions, they refused to come right out and admit that they were dating. Both Alfonso and Alfieri did make a number of veiled references to their relationship.

Real-Life Wedding Album

QUINN REDEKER (ALEX MARSHALL) divorced his wife in 1967. When he realized that he couldn't financially afford to be divorced, he remarried her one year later. The second union didn't fare any better than the first.

Mary Beth Evans (KAYLA BRADY) fell in love with Dr. Michael Schwartz pretty much at first sight. While he was visiting Los Angeles from Chicago, the two went out on a total of two dates. When it came time for him to head back to Chicago, Evans followed. Five years later, he proposed marriage wearing a suit of armor.

The first night Billy Warlock (FRANKIE BRADY) met Marcy Walker (EDEN CAPWELL, *Santa Barbara*; LIZA COLBY, *All My Children*), he was wearing jeans at a black-tie function. His relaxed mode of dress even carried into their wedding, where he wore not a tuxedo or suit, but a sweater.

Patsy Pease (KIMBERLY BRADY) met her second husband, musician Robert Norton, through a computer dating service.

Drake Hogestyn (JOHN BLACK) first met his wife Victoria when he was fifteen years old. While he was playing baseball, she and her friend rode their bikes across the field. Hogestyn and Victoria had always wanted to get married on a snowy evening. While visiting family in Connecticut during Christmas week, they decided that if it snowed on New Year's Eve, they'd get married. It snowed, so they did.

Drake and Victoria Hogestyn

While vacationing on the island of Tahiti, Lauren Koslow (KATE ROBERTS KIRIAKIS) and makeup artist Nick Schillace decided to tie the knot. In keeping with the local customs, Koslow and Schillace consulted with a tribal elder on the date and time they should be married. Although it was raining on the day they planned to wed, the elder they consulted promised that the weather would clear up at four o'clock. Trusting in his wisdom, Koslow and Schillace headed out on a catamaran to be married at sea. Just as the elder had promised, at four o'clock, the skies cleared up, and the two were married.

Scott Reeves (JAKE HOGANSEN) underwent brain surgery the night before he was to have wed Melissa Brennan (JENNIFER HORTON). A sinus infection had evolved into an abscess in his brain, which had been causing him to have seizures. Once Reeves came through the operation healthy, he and Brennan rescheduled their wedding a couple of months later. The elaborate reception they had planned was scaled down to include family and close friends. As it turned out, because Brennan had already gotten her vacation time, she actually had to work on her wedding day. Not only that, she had to drive herself to the wedding, which she did while wearing her gown. As she drove along, the veil was blowing out the window.

Before marrying Scott Reeves, Melissa Brennan came very close to marrying John Travolta's nephew Tom Fridley. The two had met while working on the teen action thriller *Summer Camp Nightmare*. They intended to get married while vacationing in Jamaica and would have done so had Brennan not come down with an unpleasant case of sun poisoning.

Patty Weaver (TRISH CLAYTON) married Jerry Birn, one of the writers for *The Young and the Restless*, where she now works. On her wedding day, she was bitten by a spider.

On December 31, 1991, Deidre Hall (DR. MARLENA EVANS) married novelist-producer Steve Sohmer at his seventeenth-century manor located just outside London, England.

Jazz saxophonist Kenny G performed at Lisa Rinna's (BILLIE REED) marriage to *L.A. Law* star Harry Hamlin.

Krista Allen (BILLIE REED) married producer Justin Moritt at the home of movie star Rob Lowe.

Following a stage performance one night, Robert Kelker-Kelly (BO BRADY) asked the audience to remain in their seats. He then invited Miriam Parrish (JAMIE CALDWELL) up onto the stage, where a banner came down from the rafters reading: *Miriam, oh Miriam, will you marry me?* In front of the whole audience, Kelker-Kelly dropped to one knee and pulled out a ring.

Family Business

AFTER THE DEATH of *Days* co-creator and executive producer Ted Corday in 1966, the reins of control passed on to his widow, Betty Corday. She stepped down in 1986 and passed those reins onto their son Ken Corday, who has served as the show's executive producer ever since.

Following in his parents' footsteps, Ken Corday (center) executive produces *Days*. Also pictured (left to right): Peggy McCay, Deidre Hall, Suzanne Rogers, Lauren Koslow, Krista Allen-Moritt, Alison Sweeney, and Jaime Lyn Bauer.

Jennifer Aniston, star of the hit NBC sitcom *Friends,* is the daughter of John Aniston, who played Victor Kiriakis for eleven years. Once when Jennifer Aniston visited her father on the set of *Search for Tomorrow,* she ran into Jane Krakowski (*Ally McBeal*'s Elaine Vassal), then a teen actress on the show, who told her about a role. John Aniston walked in to find Jennifer on the phone with his agent trying to get an audition for the role she'd just heard about.

Deidre Hall's real-life twin sister Andrea Hall-Lovell played Marlena's disturbed twin Samantha, who took over Marlena's life.

Years later, Camilla More played the villainous Gillian Forrester while her real-life twin, Carey More, played Gillian's twin, Grace. In a curious bit of recasting, after Gillian was killed off, Camilla More took over the role of Grace, and Carey More ended up leaving the show. Both actresses, it should be noted, were descended from the historical figure Sir Thomas More.

Stephen Nichols's own son Aaron played Patch during a flashback scene to his childhood. One of the stipulations Nichols had for allowing his son to work on the show was that the producers come up with something his daughter Vanessa could play as well so that she would not feel left out. The show hired her to play a victim of child abuse.

In 1981, Tammy Taylor played the role of Hope Williams. Fourteen years later, Taylor's six-year-old daughter Jenna played Hope during a flashback sequence.

Deborah Moore, who played jewel thief Danielle Stevens, is the daughter of British actor Roger Moore, best known for his roles in the TV series *The Saint* and the James Bond film series.

Peter Brown (GREG PETERS) has appeared in a number of soaps including *Days of Our Lives, The Young and the Restless,* and *The Bold and the Beautiful.* His nephew, Philip Brown, who worked as a child on *The Doris Day Show,* has also worked on a number of soaps, both daytime and primetime. Both Browns have worked on the ABC soap opera *Loving*, although their stints on the show did not overlap.

Longtime veteran John Clarke's (MICKEY HORTON) daughter Mindy joined the cast in 1989 as Faith Taylor, the daughter of a racist evangelist. Since before she started school, Mindy Clarke had wanted to act but her father forbid her to do so professionally until she turned eighteen. To give her a real feel for what show business was like, he also refused to pull any strings to help her land a role on *Days*.

Susan Seaforth Hayes's (JULIE OLSON WILLIAMS) mother Elizabeth Harrower, who worked on a number of radio soaps, took on the role of *Days* head writer during the late 1970s.

Gregg Marx, who played Julie's son David Banning, is the grandson of Gummo Marx of the famous Marx Brothers comedy team. (Gummo is the brother who appeared in the Vaudeville act, but not in their films.) That makes Gregg great-nephew to Groucho, Chico, Harpo, and Zeppo.

Shannon Sturges, who played Molly Brinker during the early 1990s, is the granddaughter of legendary film director Preston Sturges (*Sullivan's Travels*).

Jed Allan's (DON CRAIG) son Mitch Brown played Dylan Ross on the CBS soap *Capitol* in the mid-1980s.

*M*A*S*H* star Alan Alda's father Robert and his brother Antony both worked on *Days of Our Lives*. Robert Alda played radio station owner Stuart Whyland in the early 1980s. Antony joined the show ten years later as the shady Johnny Corelli.

Charles Shaughnessy's (SHANE DONOVAN) brother David is a producer at *The Young and the Restless*. Their father Alfred was a head writer on the British primetime serial *Upstairs, Downstairs*.

Alumni Newsletter

FOR THE PAST FIVE SEASONS, Charles Shaughnessy (SHANE DONOVAN) has been playing opposite Fran Drescher in the CBS sitcom *The Nanny.* Shaughnessy stars as Maxwell Sheffield, a Broadway producer who hired Drescher's character, also named Fran, to look after his children. Fran and Maxwell's slowly building romance, which climaxed with a wedding in May 1998, has at times turned the comedy series into a quasi-soap opera. The writers have also inserted a handful of inside jokes relating to Shaughnessy's background on *Days.* One first season episode found Fran and her mother watching *Days of Our Lives.* When Maxwell asked how they could watch those shows, Fran responded, "You're right. It hasn't been the same since Shane left." To that, Maxwell replied: "You know, he auditioned for me once . . . with that phony British accent."

Michael T. Weiss was the thirteenth actor to slide into the role of Dr. Mike Horton. As such, it seems somehow fitting that Weiss should now be best known for playing a character with the ability to slide in and out of other people's personalities. For the past three seasons, he has played the mysterious Jarod, the title role in NBC's primetime action series *The Pretender.*

After being replaced on *Days,* Andrea Barber, who originated the role of Carrie Brady, enjoyed a long run as the eccentric kid next door on the hit ABC sitcom *Full House.*

Leann Hunley (ANNA DiMERA) left *Days* to play Gordon Thomson's love interest on *Dynasty.* More recently, she has been seen on the WB teen

Before he was *The Nanny*'s Maxwell Sheffield,
Charles Shaughnessy played super spy Shane Donovan.

soap *Dawson's Creek* as the high school teacher who slept with one of her students.

Shannon Sturges (MOLLY BRINKER) almost didn't get the role of Reese Burton on the Aaron Spelling soap opera *Savannah* because the casting people didn't think that she was pretty enough. She turned around and showed them by being named one of *People* magazine's "50 Most Beautiful People in the World."

Joan Van Ark, who played model Janene Whitney in the early 1970s, became a TV favorite as romance novelist Valene Ewing on the *Dallas* spin-off *Knots Landing*.

The late Mary Frann, who played Neil Curtis's wife Amanda Howard, almost made the segue from daytime to primetime soap operas in the late 1970s. She came very close to landing the role of J. R. Ewing's wife Suellen on *Dallas*. Although Linda Gray snagged that role, a couple of years later, Frann ended up playing wife to comedian Bob Newhart on *Newhart*.

Amy Yasbeck (OLIVIA REED) has balanced a number of film and television roles. For three seasons, she played Crystal Bernard's younger sister on the NBC sitcom *Wings*. She has also been seen in such films as *Home for the Holidays* and the Leslie Nielsen spoof *Dracula: Dead and Loving It*.

A number of *Days* alumni have made their way from Salem Place to *Melrose Place* in the past few years. Early in the show's run, Stanley Kamel (ERIC PETERS) played the boss that Amanda Woodward (Heather Locklear) drove to suicide. The latest *Days* graduate to be seen on the show has been Steve Wilder (JACK DEVERAUX) who came on board as a fashion designer and love interest for Jane Mancini, played by Josie Bissett. Bissett's real-life husband, Rob Estes, who played Jennifer Horton's boyfriend Glenn Gallagher on *Days* in the mid-'80s, worked for several seasons on the cable crime drama *Silk Stalkings* before coming onto *Melrose* as Kyle McBride, Amanda Woodward's latest husband. Kyle's ex-wife Taylor was played by yet another *Days* alumna, Lisa Rinna (BILLIE REED). Patrick Muldoon, who played Billie's brother Austin, landed

Rob Estes (GLENN GALLAGHER), pictured here with wife and
fellow castmember Josie Bissett,
and Steve Wilder (JACK DEVERAUX), below, are two of the
Days alumni who made their way to *Melrose Place*.

the role of Richard Hart on *Melrose* almost immediately upon leaving *Days*. Muldoon has been making his way into feature films, including the sci-fi adventure *Starship Troopers*.

Richard Biggs, who played Dr. Marcus Hunter, is playing a doctor again, Stephen Franklin, on the sci-fi series *Babylon 5*. John de Lancie, whose role as inventor Eugene Bradford occasionally bordered on science fiction (robots, time machines, et cetera), is probably best known now for his recurring role in the *Star Trek* spin-offs as the seemingly omnipotent alien, Q.

De Lancie's leading lady Arleen Sorkin has been working hard in the business, even though her face isn't as prominent as it once was. She wrote the Jennifer Aniston comedy *Picture Perfect* and has provided the voice for the Joker's girlfriend, Harley Quinn, on *Batman: The Animated Series*.

Mike Farrell, who played Julie Olson's first husband Scott Banning, can now be heard as the voice of Superman's Earth father on *Superman: The Animated Series*. He is best known, however, for the role of B. J. Hunnicutt, which he played on the classic CBS sitcom *M*A*S*H* from 1975 until the series' end in 1983.

Child actor Erik Von Detten, who played Lawrence Alamain and Carly Manning's son Nicky, is carving out a promising future in show business. Since leaving *Days*, he provided the voice for Sid, the toy-abusing neighbor in Disney's computer animated hit *Toy Story*. More recently, he played Wally Cleaver in the big screen adaptation of the TV classic *Leave It to Beaver*.

Several actors have passed briefly through Salem before heading off to greater success in feature films, primetime television, or modeling. Among the day players and short-term actors who have worked on the show are Farrah Fawcett, Cindy Crawford, Pamela Anderson, Lolita Davidovich, and Kathie Lee Gifford.

Friends and Love Songs

ALTHOUGH GLORIA LORING released a number of singles and albums in the early 1970s, none had ever become hits. When she was discussing her disappointment about that fact to *Days* head writer Beth Millstein, Millstein suggested that the best way for Loring to get her hit single would be to tie it in with the show in some way. The ballad "Friends and Lovers," which was being used as a theme song for the very popular romance between Shane Donovan and Kimberly Brady, sounded like the perfect vehicle for Loring. The phones at NBC had been ringing off the hook with calls from fans wanting to know where they could buy it. The first time it was used on the show, it was performed by Jay Gruska, who had written it with his wife. Loring realized that she could perform the song herself, but that to interest a major record label in distributing it, she needed to perform it as a duet with a better established singer. She decided upon Carl Anderson, who had performed on the cast album for *Jesus Christ Superstar,* after her boyfriend at the time, Don Diamont, saw him in concert. Loring sent Anderson a tape of the song. While listening to it on his Walkman at the mall, he began to sing along. A woman stopped him to mention that it was the song from *Days of Our Lives.* That encounter convinced Anderson to record the song. His record company, however, was not interested; the company deemed the ballad too pop for Anderson, whom they were promoting as an R&B artist. Despite the fact that NBC received more calls about "Friends and Lovers" than any song from daytime or primetime until then, no major record company was interested. USA Carrere finally took a chance that paid off in spades. "Friends and Lovers" climbed all the way to number two on *Billboard's* Hot 100, and became one of the biggest singles of 1986. Since leaving *Days* that same year, Loring has released a number of albums. The title track from *Is There Anybody Out There* was used as a love song for another soap couple: Nick and Mindy on *Guiding Light*.

Bill Hayes was known as a musical performer for decades before he landed the role of singer/con man Doug Williams. Throughout the 1950s and early '60s, he released close to thirty singles and several albums. In 1955, he released "The Ballad of Davy Crockett," which climbed to number one on all the pop music charts of the day. His follow-up singles "The Legend of Wyatt Earp" and "Message from James Dean" didn't fare quite so well, but in 1957, Hayes hit the Top 40 once again with the song "Wringle Wrangle," which was used in the feature film *Westward Ho the Wagons*. In 1973, Hayes parlayed his role as Doug Williams into an album, *The Look of Love*; the title track had been heard on *Days* a number of times as Doug and Julie's theme song. Seven years later, Hayes released another album, which he titled *At Doug's Place*. His onscreen and real-life wife, Susan Seaforth Hayes, performed two duets with him on it.

Like Bill Hayes, Robert Clary (ROBERT LECLAIR) had released a number of singles and albums in the 1950s. His albums included *Meet Robert Clary, Live at the Playboy Club*, and *Gigi Sung by Robert Clary*. Among his singles were "The Night They Invented Champagne," "Heart of Paris," and "Hotter'n a Pistol." In 1967, he and his castmates from the sitcom *Hogan's Heroes* released an album: *Hogan's Heroes Sing the Best of WWII*. Clary could also be heard singing on the soundtrack to the 1975 feature film *The Hindenburg*. More recently, Clary has released two new CDs, *Robert Clary Sings at the Jazz Bakery* (1997) and *Robert Clary Sings Rodgers, Hart & Mercer* (1998).

Kaye Stevens, who played Jeri Clayton in the mid-1970s, was a popular singer-comedienne in nightclubs from Atlantic City to Las Vegas. The titles of her albums *Ruckus at the Riviera* (1961) and *Not So Great Songs That Were Left Out of Great Movies* (1963) show Stevens's gift for combining comedy and music.

Marilyn McCoo made her *Days of Our Lives* debut as Tamara Price at Marlena's 1986 marriage to John Black. At the wedding, McCoo sang "Up Where We Belong" from *An Officer and a Gentleman*. Prior to landing on *Days*, McCoo had enjoyed a successful career in music. In the late 1960s and early '70s, as part of the 5th Dimension, she had two number one hits—"Aquarius/Let the Sunshine In" and "Wedding Bell Blues"—as well as five other top ten singles: "Up, Up and Away," "Stoned Soul Picnic," "One Less Bell to Answer," "(Last Night) I Didn't Get to Sleep at All," and "If I Could Reach You." In the mid-'70s, McCoo and her husband, Billy Davis Jr., broke away from the 5th Dimension. They reached the top of the charts with their duet "You Don't Have to Be a Star (To Be in My Show)."

In the early 1980s, Tanya Boyd (CELESTE) took Marilyn McCoo's place in the 5th Dimension when it went on a national tour. Boyd, who has been blessed with the ability to hear obscure musical tones, has performed back up for such popular R&B performers as Anita Baker, Lou Rawls, and Natalie Cole.

Wally Kurth's role as Justin Kiriakis occasionally gave him the opportunity to show off his vocal abilities. Some of the most memorable and romantic moments between Justin and Adrienne (played by Judi Evans) came when Justin would serenade her. In the last few years, Kurth has released a couple of albums: *Kurth and Taylor* and *Half and Half*, the title of which refers to the fact that half the album was performed with electric guitars, the other half acoustic. Kurth's current role on *General Hospital* as businessman by day, rock star by night Ned Ashton has given Kurth the chance to perform on the show a number of songs from his albums.

Robert Mailhouse (BRIAN SCOFIELD) plays drums in the Los Angeles-based surf punk band Dogstar, most famous for its bassist, film star Keanu Reeves (*Speed, Bill and Ted's Excellent Adventure*). Mailhouse met Reeves while they were shopping in the same supermarket. Reeves, a hockey fan, commented on the hockey shirt Mailhouse was wearing, and the two struck up a conversation. Because of Reeves's fame, the band has played on national venues such as *Late Night with David Letterman*.

Charlotte Ross's role as Eve Donovan eventually gave her the opportunity to show off her vocal talents. In 1991, after leaving the show, she released *After Hours*, a collection of songs written by her former cast-mate Antony Alda (JOHNNY CORELLI). Ross can also be heard singing a solo on the cast album for *The Heights*, a short-lived Fox series on which she also starred.

Matthew Ashford (JACK DEVERAUX) released a cassette recording of covers and original music, which he titled *Something Went Right* and made available through his fan club. Among the original songs on the cassette is one titled "Diggin' the Dude on Daytime," which was written by his wife, Christina.

In 1997, Brian Lane Green (ALAN BRANDT) released a self-titled compact disk including a number of ballads, both original and covers. Among the covers he performs on it is the Roy Orbison classic "Crying."

Because of the international appeal of *The Bold and the Beautiful*, on which she starred for several years, Lauren Koslow (KATE ROBERTS KIRIAKIS) released an album in Egypt and Turkey.

Days gave Wally Kurth (JUSTIN KIRIAKIS) a chance to show off
his musical talents.

Double Duty

DEIDRE HALL (DR. MARLENA EVANS) almost didn't get the role of Jessie Witherspoon on the primetime drama *Our House* because the producers found her too glamorous. She modeled Jessie after Drake Hogestyn's mother. She managed to balance *Our House* with *Days* during the former's first season by taping her *Days* scenes on the weekends.

Josh Taylor's (CHRIS KOSITCHEK) role as Valerie Harper's husband in the NBC sitcom *Valerie* (later renamed *The Hogan Family* after Harper left the show) had him running each day from the *Days* studio to MGM, where *Valerie* filmed, back to *Days* and back to MGM again.

During the 1990–91 season, Lorenzo Caccialanza balanced his role as Victor's bodyguard Nico with a recurring role on the primetime serial *Knots Landing* as con artist Nick Schillace. Interestingly, the *Knots* character was named after Lauren Koslow's (KATE ROBERTS KIRIAKIS) husband, a makeup artist on the show.

Days could not use Arleen Sorkin (CALLIOPE JONES) on Fridays because she co-hosted the taping of America's Funniest People on those days. Prior to co-hosting *America's Funniest People*, Sorkin balanced her duties as a comic heroine on *Days* with a role as Geneva the maid in the Fox sitcom *Duet*.

Since *Melrose Place* films its scenes far ahead of their airing, Deborah Adair's (KATE ROBERTS) final episodes on the show overlapped with her first episode on *Days*. Similarly, Kristian Alfonso's (HOPE WILLIAMS BRADY) return to the show in 1990 overlapped with her last episodes of the primetime serial *Falcon Crest*.

Peggy McCay's light workload as Caroline Brady has allowed her to moonlight on the NBC primetime thriller *Profiler*.

the RUMORS OF HIS DEATH

Stefano DiMera has more than earned his nickname, the Phoenix. Since his first appearance on the show back in the early 1980s, he has risen from the dead more than any other villain on daytime. The following puzzle asks you to pick out in which of the following scenarios he was actually presumed to have died.

1. He suffered a stroke while in prison.　　　　　TRUE/FALSE

2. He suffered a fatal heart attack on the operating table
during open heart surgery.　　　　　TRUE/FALSE

3. Bo Brady knocked him off the side of a cliff.　　　　　TRUE/FALSE

4. His limo was driven into Salem River.　　　　　TRUE/FALSE

5. He was crushed to death in a trash compactor.　　　　　TRUE/FALSE

6. Dr. Marlena Evans shot him.　　　　　TRUE/FALSE

7. His car exploded after John Black shot at it.　　　　　TRUE/FALSE

8. His plane crashed in South America.　　　　　TRUE/FALSE

9. He was incinerated during a struggle with Satan.　　　　　TRUE/FALSE

10. A Parisian tunnel explosion buried him alive.　　　　　TRUE/FALSE

Finding the Inspiration

AN ADVERTISEMENT in a San Francisco newspaper caught head writer Pat Falken Smith's attention. A man was offering ten thousand dollars to any woman who would carry a child for him. From that ad evolved an artificial insemination storyline: Desperate to give his motherless daughter Hope a sibling, Doug Williams (Bill Hayes) gave his sperm to Dr. Neil Curtis with instructions to find an anonymous surrogate. Dr. Curtis subsequently impregnated Doug's own housekeeper with his sperm, setting off a complicated paternity storyline.

Producer Shelly Curtis came up with the idea for Calliope Jones while attending a Cyndi Lauper concert. In addition to hits like "Girls Just Wanna Have Fun," Lauper was well known for her outlandish wardrobe. Curtis felt that such an outrageous character could provide the show with a much-needed dose of humor. She worked with the writers to flesh out the character.

In the 1987 thriller *The Bedroom Window*, Steve Guttenberg passed himself off as an eyewitness to a murder attempt after his boss's wife, with whom he was having an affair, saw the murder attempt from her window. This plot twist surfaced on *Days* a year later during the Riverfront Knifer storyline. Frankie Brady (Billy Warlock) was having an affair with the older Paula Carson, his superior at a teen hotline. While at her home, Frankie witnessed the serial killer strike. Rather than risk revealing their affair, Frankie coached Paula so that she could tell the police what he saw as if she'd seen it herself. Head writer Leah Laiman herself had not seen the movie when one of the staffers came up with the idea.

Although made in 1963, the political thriller *The Manchurian Candidate* was not released theatrically until 1987. In the film, Frank Sinatra played a war hero who had been brainwashed into becoming an assassin for an enemy nation. The following year, head writer Leah Laiman planned her own version of the story involving the character of Shane Donovan, the British spy. During the writers' strike, however, the storyline was rewritten for John Black, who at the time thought he was Roman Brady. As usual, Stefano DiMera was behind the brainwashing and tried to get John/Roman to kill the whole Brady family.

The scene during which John Black and Diana Colville circle each other on the way to the bed before making love was consciously lifted from the Meryl Streep/Robert Redford big screen romance *Out of Africa*.

When Andrew Lloyd Webber's *Phantom of the Opera* was taking Broadway by storm, Matthew Ashford came up with the idea of creating a storyline for Jack based on the musical. While the writers liked the idea of a *Phantom* story, they wrote it for Nick Corelli, the former pimp who had fallen in love with one of his prostitutes, Eve Donovan. After being presumed killed in a car crash, a disfigured Nick roamed the streets of Salem cloaked and enchanted by Eve's newfound career as a singer. The show tried but did not receive permission to use any of Webber's music for the story.

In the late summer of 1991, *All My Children, Days'* rival for the 1:00 P.M. time slot, began a storyline in which heroine Natalie Hunter (Kate Collins) was dropped into a well by her lookalike sister Janet Green (also played by Collins), who proceeded to take over Natalie's life. As Natalie languished in the well for weeks on end, the ratings soared. *Days,* which needed a good ratings boost, introduced its own variation on the story a year later. Envious of Marlena Evans's seemingly perfect life and jealous of her husband Roger's infatuation with Marlena, Stella Lombard dropped her rival into the boiler pit of an abandoned warehouse. The storyline didn't jump-start the ratings immediately, but Marlena's imprisonment was used as a catalyst for the renewed relationship between her and John Black, which has definitely helped to increase ratings over the years.

The writers drew heavily from the classic 1970s horror film *The Exorcist* for the storyline in which Dr. Marlena Evans was possessed by Satan. Churches were desecrated, the exorcism was performed by a fallen priest, and the possessed one levitated above her bed. As Deidre Hall pointed out, in the *Days* version, she levitated both horizontally and vertically. So close were some of the effects and gimmicks to the original *Exorcist* movie that some soap columnists joked that they weren't looking forward to seeing any pea soup spit up onscreen.

Just Passing through Town

A **1984 CHARITY EVENT** not only allowed cast members like Gloria Loring (LIZ CURTIS) to show off their musical abilities, it also brought onto the show musical acts like jazz singer Al Jarreau and rock band Billy Vera and the Beaters. Among the numbers that Billy Vera and the Beaters performed was "At This Moment," which became a theme song for Kimberly Brady and Shane Donovan.

Wheel of Fortune host Pat Sajak played news reporter Kevin Hathaway in 1983, allowing for a bit of cross promotion between the soap opera and game show audiences.

Bob Eubanks, host of *The Newlywed Game,* appeared as himself when Calliope and Eugene Bradford (Arleen Sorkin and John de Lancie) competed on the game show while honeymooning in Los Angeles.

Laugh-In regular Ruth Buzzi added a touch of comic relief to the Salem Slasher mystery as Eugene Bradford's eccentric cousin Letitia who joined the unlucky list of murder victims.

When Calliope Jones inherited a minor league baseball team, the show recruited a couple of major leaguers to appear as players: Kirk McCaskill and Ron Romick from the California Angels.

In the late 1980s, NBC ran a contest in which soap fans had to spot Betty White's cameo appearance on each of its daytime soap operas. White, at the time, was starring in one of the network's most popular sitcoms, *The Golden Girls*. Her *Days* cameo took place in the Salem Police Department, where Frankie Brady (Billy Warlock) spotted her.

Talk show host Leeza Gibbons, a *Days* fan, has invited cast members onto her self-titled show and has herself guested on *Days* twice. In 1994, she played a shopper in Salem Place, whom Bo Brady and Billie Reed (Robert Kelker-Kelly and Lisa Rinna) questioned while looking for Hope (Kristian Alfonso). The scene allowed Gibbons to work with Kelker-Kelly, her favorite actor on the show and a popular guest on her own show. The following year, to celebrate the show's thirtieth anniversary, she returned as a nurse in University Hospital. That scene allowed her to work with Deidre Hall, telling Dr. Marlena Evans that she had a phone call.

Country superstar LeAnn Rimes has been watching *Days of Our Lives* for fifteen years—an especially impressive claim since she is only seventeen years old. Her history with the show began at the age of two, sitting on the lap of her grandmother, who was a fan. In late April and early May of 1998, Rimes made a three-day stop in Salem, playing a homeless teenager befriended by Eric Brady (Jensen Ackles).

Famous Fans

MOVIE STAR JULIA ROBERTS, who'd been turned down for roles on *All My Children* and *Santa Barbara*, was given a People's Choice Award as Best Actress in a Comedy for her work in the film *My Best Friend's Wedding*. During her acceptance speech, she mentioned that she was excited because the entire cast from *Days of Our Lives* was sitting in the audience.

Country singer Trisha Yearwood ("She's in Love with the Boy," "How Do I Live"), who got hooked on *Days* through her mother, can remember back to the time that Marlena's twin sister Samantha stole her life. When Yearwood entered college, she and her friends would cut classes to follow the exploits of Bo and Hope.

Beverly Hills, 90210 star Tori Spelling has long been a fan of *Days of Our Lives* as well as *Another World*. Through her makeup artist Nick Schillace, who is married to Lauren Koslow (KATE ROBERTS), Spelling has visited the *Days* set. She was also responsible for helping Patrick Muldoon (AUSTIN REED) land a pivotal role on *Melrose Place,* which is produced by her father Aaron Spelling.

Before landing the role of Hope Williams, Kristian Alfonso had worked with Rock Hudson in the TV movie *The Starmaker*. About a year after starting on *Days*, Alfonso spotted Hudson at a hamburger place. Not expecting him to remember her, she walked over to reintroduce herself. The first question out of his mouth was, "When are you going to marry Bo?"

WKRP in Cincinnati star Loni Anderson has been a longtime Days of Our Lives fan. Her former husband Burt Reynolds's dinner theater in Florida gave her the opportunity to meet a number of her favorite actors from the show. When Peter Reckell (BO BRADY) was performing there in Deathtrap, Loni not only saw the show four times, she brought friends of hers each time who loved Days and wanted to meet him. Anderson herself is a very good friend of Deidre Hall's.

Baywatch beauty Erika Eleniak's devotion to Days proved instrumental in Billy Warlock's return to the show in 1990. After Warlock moved in with Eleniak, sitting beside her while she watched the show renewed his interest in it. At one point, Eleniak mentioned to Warlock that Frankie should come back to complicate the relationship between Jack and Jennifer. A couple of weeks later, Warlock received a phone call from the show asking him if he would be interested in coming back.

Clive Cussler, bestselling author of such action novels as Vixen 03, Night Probe! and Raise the Titanic, contacted the show after watching Drake Hogestyn's dungeon scenes during the Maison Blanche storyline. Cussler wanted the name of Hogestyn's agent because he thought Hogestyn would be perfect for the role of Dirk Pitt in a film version of Raise the Titanic.

Oscar-nominated actress Cathy Moriarty (Best Supporting Actress, Raging Bull) got drawn into Days while recovering from back problems. When she filmed the big screen soap spoof Soapdish, she made a point to go over and meet Stephen Nichols (PATCH), who made a cameo appearance in it.

When gymnast Kim Zimeskal first began training for the Olympics, she stayed with another gymnast who was hooked on Days of Our Lives. It wasn't long before Zimeskal herself was caught up in the romances of Jack and Jennifer and Bo and Carly. She would watch the show to relax before heading off to the gym.

R&B singer Aaron Neville, who hit the top ten with "Tell It Like It Is" in the 1960s and more recently in a duet with Linda Ronstadt ("Don't Know

Much"), watches both *Days* and *All My Children*. When he ran into Renée Jones (LEXIE CARVER), he told her he would love to guest star on the show and maybe sing a song. He'd already gotten to serenade Susan Lucci (ERICA KANE) on *All My Children*.

One-time Hollywood leading lady Joan Blondell made more than eighty films, including *A Tree Grows in Brooklyn, The Public Enemy,* and an Oscar-nominated role in the 1951 drama *The Blue Veil.* Speaking about Susan Seaforth Hayes's performance on *Days of Our Lives,* Blondell told *Time* magazine: "I don't know anyone but Sarah Bernhardt who could sustain all that suffering so long."

Florence Henderson, best known as the mother on *The Brady Bunch,* used to tune into *Days* when she was on the road, traveling and doing musicals at night.

Deborah Harmon, who played the mother on the ABC sitcom *Just the Ten of Us* and later worked on the Judd Hirsch sitcom *Dear John,* was a fan of *Days* and of the romance between Justin Kiriakis and Adrienne Johnson in particular. JoAnn Willette, who played Harmon's daughter on *Just the Ten of Us,* went to college with Wally Kurth (JUSTIN). At Harmon's wedding, Willette surprised her onscreen mom by arranging for Kurth to serenade her. Kurth sang "In Paradise," which he had performed on the show the day that Justin asked Adrienne to marry him.

Arleen Sorkin (CALLIOPE JONES) discovered that singer Rosemary Clooney was a fan of the show when she attended the wedding of Clooney's son.

Eileen Barrett, who played Stephanie Woodruff, had a similar encounter with Caesar Romero, the former matinee idol best known for playing Joker on the 1960s *Batman* TV series. He told her that he loved Stephanie during a charity event they were both attending.

Maree Cheatham (MARIE HORTON) was thrilled to sing "The Star Spangled Banner" with opera legend Beverly Sills, who was equally thrilled to be singing it with "Marie Horton."

Jaime Lyn Bauer (DR. LAURA HORTON) learned through her husband, makeup artist Jeremy Swan, that *Honeymooners* star Audrey Meadows was a big fan of hers. Bauer got to talk to Meadows when she called the house looking for Swan.

Talk show host Jerry Springer has not only admitted to being a fan of *Days* but of Kristian Alfonso (HOPE WILLIAMS BRADY) in particular. He once picked her as the soap star he'd most like to have on his show.

According to *Time* magazine, the late Thurgood Marshall, former Supreme Court Justice, "slipped away from deliberations to ponder *Days of Our Lives.*"

Before Monica Lewinsky made headlines for her affair with President Bill Clinton, she got her name in the papers when she was quoted about the popularity of *Days of Our Lives* while at a fan club convention.

Other notable fans of the show have included film legend Jimmy Stewart, country singer Tammy Wynette, and comedienne Edie Adams.

Stars Who Were Fans Before They Joined the Cast

ALISON SWEENEY had been watching the show from a very young age. Because she had been a fan for such a long time before joining the cast, she worried that she wouldn't get used to calling the actors by their real names.

Lisa Rinna used to have a crush on Peter Reckell from watching him play Bo Brady. By the time Rinna joined the show—as Billie Reed, a love interest for Bo—Reckell had been replaced by Robert Kelker-Kelly. She had, however, gotten the chance to meet Reckell at a Hollywood function. One month before Rinna was leaving *Days,* Reckell returned to the show as Bo, giving her the chance to finally work with him.

Just like Rinna, Krista Allen-Moritt, who took over the role of Billie, also once had a crush on Peter Reckell as Bo.

Robert S. Woods, who had won an Emmy playing cowboy Bo Buchanan on ABC's *One Life to Live,* liked *Days* not only for its pacing but also for the way it took chances with rogue characters. Since he was planning on leaving *One Life* and New York to head out to California, where *Days* was filmed, he decided to let his interest in the show be known. At the 1985 Emmy Awards, he approached Shelly Curtis, who was producing the show at the time, and suggested that he come on *Days* as Chris Kositchek's brother.

Although the show did not take him up on that particular suggestion, he did wind up on *Days* the following year as Paul Stewart.

When Matt Battaglia was in college, his entire football team followed *Days of Our Lives,* often watching the show before practice. At the time Battaglia and his team were tuning in, Bo and Hope were a front-burner couple. Years later, when Battaglia joined the show as drug lord J. L. King, he caused great problems for Bo and Hope, forcing Bo to marry Hope's rival Billie Reed.

Holly Gagnier had been following *Days of Our Lives* solidly for five years before landing the role of Ivy Selejko Jannings.

Camilla Scott, who took over the role of Melissa Horton from Lisa Trusel, used to race home from school every afternoon to follow the romance between Bo and Hope. As a devoted fan, she was well acquainted with Trusel's interpretation of Melissa. To make the role more her own, Scott decided to approach Melissa as a completely new character.

Antony Alda (Johnny Corelli) first started watching *Days* back in the late 1970s when his father Robert Alda (Stuart Whyland) worked on the show. After his father left, so many of Antony Alda's friends landed roles on the show that he watched it fairly consistently until he himself was cast as Johnny Corelli.

Lark Voorhies started watching in the late 1980s. By the time she took over the role of Wendy Reardon in 1993, her favorite couple, Patch and Kayla (Stephen Nichols and Mary Beth Evans) had already left the show along with many of her other favorites.

When Miriam Parrish (Jamie Caldwell) first moved to Los Angeles, she lived with an aunt who was a diehard fan of both *Days of Our Lives* and *Another World.* It didn't take too long for Parrish to get hooked on them as well.

Bryan Dattilo picked up his *Days of Our Lives* habit from his grandmother, who had only one rule for him while he was watching with her—no talking during the show. Of course, he'd break that rule over and over again, asking the backgrounds on all the characters in a scene. While his favorite character was John Black, he developed a crush on Melissa Reeves (JENNIFER HORTON), who would become his onscreen sister. Dattilo and his grandmother are not the only *Days* fans in his family. One of his aunts scheduled her caesarian section for after that day's episode of the show.

Like Dattilo, Renée Jones (LEXIE CARVER) also used to watch *Days* with her grandmother.

When Adam Caine (EDMUND CRUMB) first arrived in the United States from England, he watched both *Days of Our Lives* and *The Young and the Restless* to familiarize himself with American television.

Katherine Ellis (TAYLOR) has been watching *Days* since she was five years old. Being such a fan of the show for so long kept her from feeling too nervous when she started working there. She told *Soap Opera Digest,* "On my first day . . . I looked around and there were all these familiar faces."

As a *Days* fan, Krista Allen-Moritt (BILLIE REED) once had a crush on Peter Reckell.

ℱan Stories

WHEN JULIE OLSON was considering whether or not to have an abortion, pro-life fans mailed in pictures of fetuses to Susan Seaforth Hayes.

While having an ice cream at the local mall, Seaforth Hayes was approached by a woman who asked if she was indeed Susan Seaforth Hayes. When Seaforth Hayes replied affirmatively, the woman responded, "Well, I'm very relieved. I just got out of the hospital, and I've been on a lot of drugs, and I thought that you weren't [her]." With that, the woman walked away.

When Wayne Northrop (ROMAN BRADY) began on *Days*, his phone number was still listed with directory information. He finally decided to have it changed to an unlisted number after fans from around the country kept not only calling him, but calling collect.

When Hope was forced into getting engaged to the slimy Larry Welch (Andrew Massett), one fan sent Kristian Alfonso a snake bite kit. During that storyline, Massett received a death threat from an inmate in a West Virginia penitentiary. After the FBI was called into the case, the prisoner sent Massett a letter of apology.

After Jack Deveraux (as played by Matthew Ashford) raped his wife, Kayla, a waitress refused to serve Ashford in a restaurant. Another fan not only found out where Ashford lived, she moved into an apartment on his street to keep tabs on "Jack."

After Darby Hinton landed the role of Ian Griffith on the show, the tellers at his bank would fight over who got to take care of him.

Leann Hunley was hired as a spokesperson for Mustang Auto because the only original member of the Ford family left on the board was a big fan of her work as Anna DiMera.

Stephen Nichols (STEVE "PATCH" JOHNSON) was surprised at how many fans did not recognize him without his character's trademark eye patch.

A couple of women were so taken with the romance between Kayla Brady (Mary Beth Evans) and Steve "Patch" Johnson (Stephen Nichols) that they believed the actors should become involved with each other in real life. The onscreen chemistry was too strong, they felt, for it not to be pursued. The women formed a fan club whose main purpose was to promote rumors that Evans and Nichols were dating, in an effort to put the bug in their ears and make it come true.

Two fans tried to push Stephen Nichols and Mary Beth Evans (STEVE "PATCH" JOHNSON and KAYLA BRADY) into a real-life romance.

Early in Melissa Reeves's tenure on *Days,* Jennifer Horton was a bit of a troublemaker. At one point, Jennifer stole the answers to an upcoming test. The plotline encouraged a high school student in Iowa to do the same thing. When the student came to regret her decision, she wrote to Melissa Reeves asking for advice. Reeves convinced the young woman to confess.

Michael Easton rejected everything the wardrobe people offered him. He wore only his own clothes on the set because it helped him to better connect with his character, Tanner Scofield. His clothing of choice included a number of jeans ripped in places where the audience could see his boxer shorts. He soon began receiving boxers in the mail from fans who wanted him to wear the shorts on air.

Years earlier, the character of Calliope Jones had become so famous for her outlandish fashion accessories that each week Arleen Sorkin received at least two pairs of novelty earrings to wear on camera.

Susan Banks (Eileen Davidson) was easily the most outlandishly wardrobed character since Calliope wore an Easter basket for her hat. So recognizable was her mode of dress that Susan became a popular costume for *Days* fans on Halloween 1997.

At one charity auction, the bidding climbed up to four hundred dollars for a towel, still damp, that Drake Hogestyn had used to dry himself off after a shower that morning.

One fan was so taken with the dress Carly Manning wore when she married Victor Kiriakis that she persuaded Richard Bloore, the dress designer, to send her his sketches. As the bride-to-be had the dress made, she would send back pictures to ask Bloore for advice on its progress.

One twelve-year-old fan of the show starting calling up tabloid newspapers such as *The Globe* and *The National Enquirer* claiming that she was a student at Princeton College who was engaged to Bryan Dattilo. She was not the only lovesick fan Dattilo has had to deal with. One woman from Canada sent him a letter saying that she had left her husband to be with him. Making that situation even worse, the woman's children wrote to him, hoping that he would be their new father.

Sometimes real friendship has developed between fans and cast members. Susan Seaforth Hayes answered a letter she received from a female police officer who was heading off to fight in Desert Storm. While the woman was overseas, Seaforth Hayes kept up the correspondence. When the woman broke her ankle and had to be sent home, Seaforth Hayes invited her to recuperate at her house. Seaforth Hayes even arranged for the woman to appear in uniform on *Days*.

One particularly devoted fan legally changed her first name to DiMera.

After following the Satanic possession storyline, one fan was unnerved by an inexplicable bad odor in her home. Just to be on the safe side, she brought in a priest to perform an exorcism.

The Daytime Emmy Awards

I N 1968, Macdonald Carey (DR. TOM HORTON) was nominated for an Emmy in the category of Individual Achievement in Daytime Drama, along with Joan Bennett from *Dark Shadows* and Celeste Holm, who had worked on the Sunday morning religious series *Insight*. Because the category was an area award, as many as all or as few as none of the nominees could be given statues. As it turned out, none of the three went home with an Emmy that night.

In 1973, Carey was nominated again, this time for Outstanding Achievement by an Individual in Daytime Drama. The all-encompassing nature of the category pitted Carey not only against a soap actress—*All My Children's* Mary Fickett, who won—but against four directors (including *Days'* own H. Wesley Kenney), a scenic designer, and a set decorator as well. The show itself was nominated for Outstanding Program Achievement in Daytime.

The following year, the Daytime Emmys were presented in their own ceremony, separate from the primetime awards. Actors, actresses, writers, directors, and technical people competed in their own categories. While *Days* fared pretty well in those early years, from the early 1980s on, the Emmys, especially those in the non-technical categories, have come few and far between. Some have speculated that *Days'* lack of Emmy nominations has been a knee-jerk reaction to the show's faring so incredibly well at the *Soap Opera Digest* Awards.

(Note: For space considerations, in the technical categories, only winners are listed below; not nominees.)

the 1974 DAYTIME EMMY AWARDS

H. Wesley Kenney picked up three Emmys. In addition to winning the award as Best Director for his work on *Days of Our Lives,* he was also named Best Individual Director for a Special Program and Daytime Director of the Year for his work on the *ABC Afternoon Playbreak* special, "Miss Kline, We Love You."

Emmys

Best Actor: Macdonald Carey (DR. TOM HORTON)

Best Individual Director: H. Wesley Kenney

Outstanding Sound Mixing

Nominations

Outstanding Drama Series

the 1975 DAYTIME EMMY AWARDS

Bill Bell, who served as head writer for *The Young and the Restless* while continuing to work on *Days of Our Lives,* earned two nominations in the writing category. He lost to the category's third nominee, the writing team from *Another World.* For the only time in the history of the Daytime Emmys, the Outstanding Actor and Actress came from the same show. Macdonald Carey became the first actor to win back-to-back Emmys; Susan Flannery used her win to wrangle some time off to film the movie *The Towering Inferno. Days of Our Lives* lost the Outstanding Drama Series Emmy to *The Young and the Restless,* which had been created by *Days'* head writer Bill Bell.

Macdonald Carey (pictured here with *Father Knows Best* star Jane Wyatt) won back-to-back Daytime Emmys.

Emmys

Outstanding Actor: Macdonald Carey (DR. TOM HORTON)

Outstanding Actress: Susan Flannery (DR. LAURA HORTON)

Nominations

Outstanding Daytime Drama Series

Outstanding Actor: Bill Hayes (DOUG WILLIAMS)

Outstanding Actress: Susan Seaforth Hayes (JULIE OLSON)

Outstanding Individual Director: Joseph Behar

Outstanding Writing

the 1976 DAYTIME EMMY AWARDS

Once again, Bill Bell found himself double nominated in the Outstanding Writing category. This time, however, he won, for *Days*. One-time onscreen rivals Susan Seaforth Hayes and Denise Alexander (now on *General Hospital*) found themselves in competition for the Outstanding Actress Emmy, but both lost to Helen Gallagher of *Ryan's Hope*. *Time* magazine had predicted an easy win for Seaforth Hayes.

Emmys
Outstanding Writing

Nominations
Outstanding Daytime Drama Series

Outstanding Actor: Macdonald Carey (DR. TOM HORTON) and
Bill Hayes (DOUG WILLIAMS)

Outstanding Actress: Susan Seaforth Hayes (JULIE OLSON)

the 1977 DAYTIME EMMY AWARDS

For the first time, two directors from the same show competed against each other: *Days*' Joseph Behar and Al Rabin. Neither won.

Nominations
Outstanding Daytime Drama Series

Outstanding Individual Director: Joseph Behar and Al Rabin

Outstanding Writing

the 1978 DAYTIME EMMY AWARDS

For the first and only time to date, *Days of Our Lives* was named Best Show.

Emmys
Outstanding Daytime Series

Outstanding Actress: Susan Seaforth Hayes (JULIE WILLIAMS)

Outstanding Individual Director: Al Rabin

Outstanding Writing

the 1979 DAYTIME EMMY AWARDS

The first Daytime Emmys in supporting categories were awarded. Suzanne Rogers won, beating out her castmate Frances Reid. During Rogers's acceptance speech, she thanked only her leading man, John Clarke. While Rogers had been nominated in the Supporting Actress category, Clarke had been nominated in the lead category. Rogers and Peter Hansen (LEE BALDWIN, *General Hospital*), who picked up the Emmy as Best Supporting Actor, both won their awards for alcoholism stories. Writer Elizabeth Harrower competed against herself—she was nominated for her work on both *Days of Our Lives* and *The Young and the Restless*—but won for neither category.

Emmys

Outstanding Supporting Actress: Suzanne Rogers (MAGGIE HORTON)

Nominations

Outstanding Daytime Drama

Outstanding Actor: Jed Allan (DON CRAIG) and
John Clarke (MICKEY HORTON)

Outstanding Actress: Susan Seaforth Hayes (JULIE WILLIAMS)

Outstanding Supporting Actor: Joseph Gallison (DR. NEIL CURTIS)

Outstanding Supporting Actress: Frances Reid (ALICE HORTON)

Outstanding Direction

Outstanding Writing

the 1980 DAYTIME EMMY AWARDS

Despite being one of the show's leading ladies, Deidre Hall's first Emmy nomination came not in a lead but in a supporting category. Hugh McPhillips, who had directed *The Doctors* for many years, beat out such name stars as Oscar winner Joan Fontaine and Mr. Entertainment Sammy Davis Jr. for the one time only category Outstanding Cameo Appearance.

Emmys
Outstanding Cameo Appearance: Hugh McPhillips (HUGH PEARSON)

Nominations
Outstanding Supporting Actress: Deidre Hall (DR. MARLENA EVANS)

the 1981 AND 1982 DAYTIME EMMY AWARDS

Amidst a heavy bias toward the ABC soaps, *Days of Our Lives* was completely shut out of the Emmys for two years.

the 1983 DAYTIME EMMY AWARDS

In response to NBC receiving so few Emmy nominations, the network, whose turn it was to broadcast the awards ceremony, declined to do so. Although the ceremony's poor ratings potential was blamed, most industry pundits agreed that NBC simply didn't want to be promoting a rival network. *Days of Our Lives* managed to grab a nomination for Outstanding Daytime Drama Series without pulling down a single other nomination in any of the acting, writing, directing, or technical categories.

Nominations
Outstanding Daytime Drama

the 1984 DAYTIME EMMY AWARDS

NBC not only declined to broadcast the ceremony again, the network also refused to participate in the nomination or election process, claiming that there were problems with the balloting procedure. Despite the NBC boycott, *Days* racked up three times as many nominations as it had the previous year.

Nominations

Outstanding Daytime Drama Series

Outstanding Actress: Deidre Hall (DR. MARLENA EVANS BRADY)

Outstanding Writing

the 1985 DAYTIME EMMY AWARDS

For the first time, younger actors and actresses were nominated in categories of their own. Castmates Kristian Alfonso and Lisa Trusel competed for Best Ingenue but lost to former *Days* cast member Tracey E. Bregman, who won for her work on *The Young and the Restless*.

Nominations

Outstanding Daytime Drama Series

Outstanding Actress: Deidre Hall (DR. MARLENA EVANS BRADY)

Outstanding Ingenue: Kristian Alfonso (HOPE WILLIAMS BRADY) and
Lisa Trusel (MELISSA ANDERSON)

Outstanding Direction

Outstanding Writing

the 1986 DAYTIME EMMY AWARDS

Not only had Leann Hunley already left *Days* when she won the Best Supporting Actress Emmy, she was filming an episode of *Hotel* on the day of the ceremony, so she couldn't even pick it up.

Emmys

Outstanding Supporting Actress: Leann Hunley (ANNA DiMERA)

Nominations

Outstanding Actress: Peggy McCay (CAROLINE BRADY)

Outstanding Direction

the 1987 DAYTIME EMMY AWARDS

While it has become commonplace for lead actors and actresses to better their chances of winning by submitting their names in the supporting categories, rarely does a supporting player garner a nomination in a lead category. Frances Reid, on the basis of her longevity with the show, managed to earn a Best Actress nomination for what has historically been a supporting role.

Nominations

Outstanding Actress: Frances Reid (ALICE HORTON)

Outstanding Supporting Actress: Peggy McCay (CAROLINE BRADY)

Outstanding Younger Leading Man: Billy Warlock (FRANKIE BRADY)

Outstanding Direction

Outstanding Writing

the 1988 DAYTIME EMMY AWARDS

Billy Warlock's Emmy as Outstanding Younger Leading Man would be the last non-technical Emmy *Days* would receive for more than ten years and counting. The following year, Warlock's ex-wife Marcy Walker would win the Outstanding Lead Actress Emmy for her work on *Santa Barbara*. Joe Behar, who worked on both *Days of Our Lives* and the courtroom anthology series *Superior Court*, competed against himself in the category of Outstanding Drama Series Directing Team, but didn't win either award.

Emmys

Outstanding Younger Leading Man: Billy Warlock (FRANKIE BRADY)

Outstanding Achievement in Makeup

Outstanding Achievement in Hairstyling

Outstanding Achievement in Costume Design

Nominations

Outstanding Lead Actor: Stephen Nichols (STEVE "PATCH" JOHNSON)

Outstanding Supporting Actress: Arleen Sorkin (CALLIOPE JONES)

the 1989 DAYTIME EMMY AWARDS

Hearing-impaired Darryl Utley became the first physically challenged soap actor to earn a Daytime Emmy nomination.

Nominations

Outstanding Supporting Actor: Joseph Campanella (HARPER DEVERAUX)

Outstanding Supporting Actress: Jane Elliot (ANJELICA DEVERAUX) and Arleen Sorkin (CALLIOPE JONES)

Outstanding Juvenile Male: Darryl Utley (BENJY DIMERA)

the 1990 DAYTIME EMMY AWARDS

Although *Days* was often praised for its use of contemporary music throughout the 1970s and '80s, the show received its only Emmy in a music category in 1990.

Emmys

Outstanding Musical Direction and Composition

Nominations

Outstanding Juvenile Female: Charlotte Ross (EVE DONOVAN)

the 1991 DAYTIME EMMYS

James Reynolds, who had played Abe Carver throughout the 1980s without any Emmy recognition, was nominated as Best Actor when he took over the role of Henry Marshall on *Generations*. Charlotte Ross lost the Outstanding Younger Actress Emmy to future movie star Anne Heche.

Emmys
Outstanding Makeup

Nominations
Outstanding Younger Actress: Charlotte Ross (EVE DONOVAN)

the 1992 DAYTIME EMMYS

Bill Bell was presented with the Lifetime Achievement Award for his contributions to daytime, including his tenure as head writer on *Days of Our Lives*. Outstanding Younger Actress nominee Melissa Reeves (JENNIFER HORTON) lost out to her real-life husband's leading lady Tricia Cast (NINA WEBSTER, *The Young and the Restless*). Macdonald Carey came under fire when, in reference to the red AIDS ribbons the celebrities were wearing, he off-handedly and with no offense intended joked, "Better dead than red."

Emmys
Outstanding Makeup

Nominations
Outstanding Younger Actress: Melissa Reeves (JENNIFER HORTON)

the 1993 DAYTIME EMMY AWARDS

A four-year dry spell for acting nominations began for *Days*.

Nominations
Outstanding Directing Team

the 1994 DAYTIME EMMY AWARDS

Susan Lucci co-hosted the ceremony for a third year in a row, sharing the stage with leading men from all three networks. Drake Hogestyn (JOHN BLACK) represented NBC. At the time the Emmys were to take place, Hogestyn's character was chained up in Stefano DiMera's dungeon and had grown a rather thick beard. NBC did not want an unshaven Hogestyn hosting the Emmys, so—despite Hogestyn's complaints—the writers threw together a scene in which Stefano had John shaved.

Nominations
Outstanding Writing Team

the 1995 DAYTIME EMMY AWARDS

Deidre Hall (MARLENA EVANS), Robert Kelker-Kelly (BO BRADY), and talk show host (and *Days* fan) Leeza Gibbons co-hosted the ceremony. *Friends* star Jennifer Aniston presented an award with her real-life father John Aniston (VICTOR KIRIAKIS). *Days of Our Lives* co-creator Ted Corday and his wife Betty, who executive produced the show for twenty years, were post-humously recognized with a Lifetime Achievement Award. Their son, current executive producer Ken Corday, accepted the award on their behalf.

Emmys
Outstanding Hairstyling

Nominations
Outstanding Daytime Drama

the 1996 DAYTIME EMMY AWARDS

For years, Deidre Hall refrained from entering herself into consideration for an Emmy. She reasoned that she might receive a nomination on the basis of her name alone, a nomination that might rightfully belong to a more deserving but lesser known actress. Hall considered her performance in the Satanic possession storyline, though, worthy of a nomination. Not only did she enter her name for consideration, she mailed out videotapes containing scenes from her storyline to actors outside her show. Although she was not the first or only performer to openly campaign for a nomination, Hall was widely criticized for her self-promotion, which was frowned on by the Academy of Television Arts & Sciences as well. Even worse, she didn't get the nomination.

*N*ominations

Outstanding Drama

Outstanding Directing Team

the 1997 DAYTIME EMMY AWARDS

When *Days* was nominated for Best Show, the producers submitted the episodes that took place in the Paris underground, which found John Black almost decapitated by a guillotine. Not only did *Days* not win the Emmy, members of the Blue Ribbon panel (which votes on the Daytime Emmys) reportedly laughed during the screening. Only four actresses instead of the standard five received nominations in the category of Outstanding Actress. According to the Academy, three actresses received an equal number of votes to have qualified them for the fifth spot. Although seven performers have been nominated in one category before, the Academy chose to limit the number this year to four. Among the actresses rumored to have been deprived of a nomination was Eileen Davidson.

*E*mmys

Outstanding Music Direction and Composition

Outstanding Makeup

Outstanding Hairstyling

Outstanding Art Direction/Set Decoration/Scenic Design

Eileen Davidson's showcase performance as four characters earned her a 1998 Emmy nomination for Best Actress.

Outstanding Drama Series

Outstanding Younger Actress: Christie Clark (CARRIE BRADY)

Outstanding Directing Team

Outstanding Writing Team

the 1998 DAYTIME EMMY AWARDS

Eileen Davidson received an Emmy nomination this year as Outstanding Actress. Although she played four different characters during the eligibility period, she only submitted tapes containing scenes featuring Kristen and Susan Banks. Peter Reckell (BO BRADY) co-hosted the event with Leeza Gibbons and actors from *Another World* and *Sunset Beach*.

Nominations

Outstanding Drama Series

Outstanding Lead Actress in a Drama Series:
Eileen Davidson (KRISTEN BLAKE and SUSAN BANKS)

Outstanding Younger Actress in a Drama Series:
Christie Clark (CARRIE BRADY)

Outstanding Younger Actor in a Drama Series:
Jensen Ackles (ERIC BRADY)

Outstanding Drama Series Directing Team

Outstanding Drama Series Writing Team

The Soap Opera Digest Awards

OVER THE YEARS, the *Soap Opera Digest* Awards have been called the Soapys, the *Soap Opera Digest* Awards, and, most recently, the Soap Opera Awards. Some critics of the show have also dubbed the ceremony the *Days of Our Lives* Fan Club Awards—a jab at the fact that *Days* has won the lion's share of statuettes over the years. Since 1984, *Days of Our Lives* has won almost every award for which it has been nominated. The show has, in fact, been honored as Outstanding Daytime Drama fifteen times over the years. Fueling the dissension against *Days* have been stories of fan club members bloc voting on awards to ensure that certain performers win the prize. In an effort to more evenly distribute the awards, the editors have changed the voting procedure. In the beginning, the magazine's readers would simply vote for whomever they desired in each category. Now the list of nominees, chosen by the editors, has been trimmed down to a maximum of three per category.

the 1977 SOAPY AWARD WINNERS

Favorite Soap Opera: *Days of Our Lives*

Favorite Actor: Bill Hayes (DOUG WILLIAMS)

Favorite Actress: Susan Seaforth Hayes (JULIE WILLIAMS)

the 1978 Soapy Award Winners

Deidre Hall's twin sister, Andrea Hall-Lovell, who played her twin sister on *Days,* picked up the award as favorite newcomer. She and Deidre Hall (who would begin a winning streak as Best Actress in the early 1980s) remain the only pair of siblings to win *Soap Opera Digest* awards.

Favorite Soap Opera: *Days of Our Lives*

Favorite Actor: Jed Allan (Don Craig)

Favorite Male Newcomer: Josh Taylor (Chris Kositchek)

Favorite Female Newcomer: Andrea Hall-Lovell (Samantha Evans)

Favorite Mature Actor: Macdonald Carey (Dr. Tom Horton)

Favorite Mature Actress: Frances Reid (Alice Horton)

the 1979 Soapy Award Winners

Jed Allan, named Favorite Leading Man, and Macdonald Carey and Frances Reid, named Favorite Mature Actor and Actress, became the first performers to pick up back-to-back Soapy Awards.

Favorite Soap Opera: *Days of Our Lives*

Favorite Actor: Jed Allan (Don Craig)

Favorite Female Newcomer: Tracey Bregman (Donna Temple)

Favorite Mature Actor: Macdonald Carey (Dr. Tom Horton)

Favorite Mature Actress: Frances Reid (Alice Horton)

the 1980 and 1981 Soapy Award Winners

Days of Our Lives was completely shut out by ABC, led by *General Hospital*.

the 1982 SOAPY AWARD WINNERS

While *General Hospital* continued its winning sweep, Deidre Hall managed to pick up the award for Favorite Actress.

Favorite Actress: Deidre Hall (DR. MARLENA EVANS)

the 1983 SOAPY AWARD WINNERS

Deidre Hall managed to crack *General Hospital's* stranglehold to win her second Outstanding Actress award. Also winning from *Days* was Hall's ex-boyfriend Quinn Redeker.

Outstanding Actress: Deidre Hall (DR. MARLENA EVANS)

Favorite Villain: Quinn Redeker (ALEX MARSHALL)

the 1984 SOAP OPERA AWARDS

General Hospital's winning streak ended as *Days of Our Lives* came back strong, picking up eleven of the thirteen awards presented. Not only did *Soap Opera Digest* change the names of the awards, it also listed the first and second runners-up as well.

Outstanding Daytime Soap: *Days of Our Lives*

Outstanding Actor in a Daytime Soap: Peter Reckell (BO BRADY)

1st Runner-Up: Wayne Northrop (ROMAN BRADY)

Outstanding Actress in a Daytime Soap: Deidre Hall (DR. MARLENA EVANS)

1st Runner-Up: Kristian Alfonso (HOPE WILLIAMS)

Exciting New Actor in a Daytime Soap Opera:
Michael Leon (PETE JANNINGS)

Exciting New Actress in a Daytime Soap Opera:
Kristian Alfonso (HOPE WILLIAMS)

1st Runner-Up: Lisa Trusel (MELISSA ANDERSON)

Outstanding Youth Actor in a Daytime Soap Opera,
2nd Runner-Up: Dickie Billingsley (SCOTTY BANNING)

Outstanding Youth Actress in a Daytime Soap Opera:
Andrea Barber (CARRIE BRADY)

Outstanding Actor in a Mature Role in a Daytime Soap Opera:
Macdonald Carey (DR. TOM HORTON)

Outstanding Actress in a Mature Role in a Daytime Soap Opera:
Frances Reid (ALICE HORTON)

Outstanding Actor in a Supporting Role in a Daytime Soap Opera:
John de Lancie (EUGENE BRADFORD)

1st Runner-Up: Michael Leon (PETE JANNINGS)

Outstanding Actress in a Supporting Role:
Lisa Trusel (MELISSA ANDERSON)

1st Runner-Up: Anne-Marie Martin (GWEN DAVIES)

Outstanding Villain: Joseph Mascolo (STEFANO DIMERA)

1st Runner-Up: Quinn Redeker (ALEX MARSHALL)

the 1985 SOAP OPERA AWARDS

Days of Our Lives outdid its performance of the year before by sweeping
every single category. Arleen Sorkin (CALLIOPE JONES) became the first
performer to win two awards in the same year, Exciting New Actress and
Outstanding Actress in a Supporting Role. Instead of listing two runners-
up, *Soap Opera Digest* listed four runners-up this year. The Editor's Award
for Continuing Contribution to Daytime Drama, which was not voted on
by the fans but rather by the magazine's editors, was given to Bill Bell,
whose job as head writer had saved *Days* from extinction back in the
1960s, and who went on to create *The Young and the Restless.*

Outstanding Daytime Serial: *Days of Our Lives*

Outstanding Actor: Peter Reckell (BO BRADY)

3rd place: Wayne Northrop (ROMAN BRADY)

4th place: Charles Shaughnessy (SHANE DONOVAN)

Outstanding Actress: Deidre Hall (DR. MARLENA EVANS)

2nd place: Kristian Alfonso (HOPE WILLIAMS)

Outstanding Actor in a Supporting Role:
John de Lancie (EUGENE BRADFORD)

2nd place: Josh Taylor (CHRIS KOSITCHEK)

Outstanding Actress in a Supporting Role:
Arleen Sorkin (CALLIOPE JONES)

2nd place: Frances Reid (ALICE HORTON)

3rd place: Anne-Marie Martin (GWEN DAVIES)

Outstanding Villain: Joseph Mascolo (STEFANO DIMERA)

2nd place: Quinn Redeker (ALEX MARSHALL)

Outstanding Villainess: Cheryl-Ann Wilson (MEGAN HATHAWAY)

3rd place: Elaine Princi (LINDA ANDERSON)

Outstanding Actor in a Mature Role:
Macdonald Carey (DR. TOM HORTON)

Outstanding Actress in a Mature Role: Frances Reid (ALICE HORTON)

Outstanding Youth Actor: Brian Autenrieth (ZACH PARKER)

Outstanding Youth Actress: Andrea Barber (CARRIE BRADY)

2nd place: Samantha Barrows (NOEL CURTIS)

Exciting New Actor: Charles Shaughnessy (SHANE DONOVAN)

Exciting New Actress: Arleen Sorkin (CALLIOPE JONES)

the 1986 SOAP OPERA AWARDS

Because of *Days'* incredible sweep the year before, the editors narrowed the potential winners to a list of nominees from which the readers could then vote. This helped to better distribute the awards, but *Days* still dominated the ceremony. In the newly instituted category of Outstanding Comic Relief, which was not gender specific, Arleen Sorkin (CALLIOPE JONES) beat out her leading man John de Lancie (EUGENE BRADFORD) as well as her cast-mate Leann Hunley (ANNA DIMERA). Bo and Hope were beaten out for Favorite Supercouple by Kimberly and Shane, whose onscreen romance had picked up heat. For the first and only time, the fans were allowed to vote on the ceremony's prestige award, Outstanding Contribution by an Actor/Actress to the Form of Continuing Drama Who Is Currently on a Daytime Serial. Deidre Hall won the award, which was presented to her by her former leading man, Wayne Northrop (ROMAN BRADY).

Winners

Outstanding Daytime Serial: *Days of Our Lives*

Outstanding Lead Actor: John Aniston (VICTOR KIRIAKIS)

Outstanding Lead Actress: Patsy Pease (KIMBERLY BRADY)

Outstanding Actor in a Supporting Role:
Stephen Nichols (STEVE "PATCH" JOHNSON)

Outstanding Young Leading Actor: Peter Reckell (BO BRADY)

Outstanding Villain: John Aniston (VICTOR KIRIAKIS)

Outstanding Comic Relief: Arleen Sorkin (CALLIOPE JONES)

Favorite Supercouple: Patsy Pease and Charles Shaughnessy
(KIMBERLY BRADY and SHANE DONOVAN)

Nominees

Outstanding Actor in a Supporting Role: Josh Taylor (CHRIS KOSITCHEK)

Outstanding Comic Relief: John de Lancie (EUGENE BRADFORD)
and Leann Hunley (ANNA DIMERA)

Favorite Supercouple: Peter Reckell and Kristian Alfonso
(BO BRADY and HOPE WILLIAMS)

the 1988 SOAP OPERA AWARDS

No *Soap Opera Digest* Awards were presented in 1987 so that the ceremony could be shifted from an end of the year event to a beginning of the year event. While *Days* did not win in every category, it did win in every category in which it was nominated. Among the four soap opera couples hosting this year's ceremony were Drake Hogestyn and Genie Francis (ROMAN BRADY and DIANA COLVILLE).

Winners

Outstanding Daytime Soap: *Days of Our Lives*

Outstanding Lead Actor: Stephen Nichols (STEVE "PATCH" JOHNSON)

Outstanding Comic Actor: Michael T. Weiss (DR. MIKE HORTON)

Outstanding Comic Actress: Arleen Sorkin (CALLIOPE JONES)

Favorite Supercouple: Charles Shaughnessy and Patsy Pease
(SHANE DONOVAN and KIMBERLY BRADY)

the 1989 SOAP OPERA AWARDS

Stephen Nichols won his third and fourth awards in his third and fourth categories. In 1987, he was Outstanding Supporting Actor; in 1988, Outstanding Actor; and this year, Outstanding Hero and half of the Favorite Supercouple. Quinn Redeker, who had previously won a *Soap Opera Digest* award for his work on *Days* picked up the Best Supporting Actor Award for his role as Rex Sterling on *The Young and the Restless*.

Winners

Outstanding Daytime Soap: *Days of Our Lives*

Outstanding Hero: Stephen Nichols (STEVE "PATCH" JOHNSON)

Outstanding Supporting Actress: Joy Garrett (JO JOHNSON)

Outstanding Villain: Matthew Ashford (JACK DEVERAUX)

Favorite Supercouple: Stephen Nichols and Mary Beth Evans
(STEVE "PATCH" JOHNSON and KAYLA BRADY)

the 1990 Soap Opera Awards

Days of Our Lives was nearly shut out by its fellow NBC soap, *Santa Barbara*, which won eight awards, including Outstanding Show. Jane Elliot, named Outstanding Villainess for her work as Anjelica Deveraux, won the show's only award. The only other *Days* performers nominated were Favorite Supercouple candidates Stephen Nichols/Mary Beth Evans and Charles Shaughnessy/Patsy Pease. Macdonald Carey and Frances Reid (Dr. Tom and Alice Horton), however, were presented with the Editor's Awards for Outstanding Contribution to Daytime.

Winners

Outstanding Villainess: Jane Elliot (Anjelica Deveraux)

Nominees

Outstanding Supercouple: Stephen Nichols and Mary Beth Evans (Steve "Patch" Johnson and and Kayla Brady); and Charles Shaughnessy and Patsy Pease (Shane Donovan and Kimberly Brady)

the 1991 Soap Opera Awards

Days of Our Lives was once again chosen as Outstanding Daytime Drama, but it only managed to win only one other award, Best Supercouple.

Winners

Outstanding Daytime Soap: *Days of Our Lives*

Outstanding Supercouple: Matthew Ashford and Melissa Reeves (Jack Deveraux and Jennifer Horton)

Nominees

Outstanding Hero: Charles Shaughnessy (Shane Donovan)

the 1992 *Soap Opera Digest* Awards

Because the Daytime Emmy Awards had fared so well in primetime the previous summer, NBC aired the *Soap Opera Digest* awards in primetime as well. Deidre Hall (DR. MARLENA EVANS) co-hosted the show with George Hamilton. Matthew Ashford and Melissa Reeves (JACK and JENNIFER) picked up a pair of awards for Best Love Story and Best Wedding. Former *Days* head writer Bill Bell picked up his second Editor's Award. Among the actresses who paid tribute to him was Susan Seaforth Hayes (JULIE OLSON WILLIAMS).

Winners
Outstanding Daytime Soap: *Days of Our Lives*

Outstanding Comic Performance: Robert Mailhouse (BRIAN SCOFIELD)

Best Wedding: Matthew Ashford and Melissa Reeves
(JACK DEVERAUX and JENNIFER HORTON)

Best Love Story: Matthew Ashford and Melissa Reeves
(JACK DEVERAUX and JENNIFER HORTON)

Nominees
Outstanding Lead Actor: Charles Shaughnessy (SHANE DONOVAN)

the 1993 *SOAP OPERA DIGEST* AWARDS

Deidre Hall once again co-hosted the evening, this time with *Mad About You* star Paul Reiser. Matthew Ashford, who had picked up the 1989 Best Villain award won this year as Outstanding Comic Relief. Hall, it should be noted, was criticized for refusing to wear a red AIDS ribbon on her dress.

Winners
Outstanding Daytime Soap: *Days of Our Lives*

Outstanding Supporting Actor: Richard Biggs (DR. MARCUS HUNTER)

Outstanding Comic Performance: Matthew Ashford (JACK DEVERAUX)

Hottest Female Star: Crystal Chappell (CARLY MANNING)

Favorite Song: "One Dream" (Bo and Carly's theme)

Outstanding Villain/Villainess: Michael Sabatino (LAWRENCE ALAMAIN)
and Louise Sorel (VIVIAN ALAMAIN)

Hottest Male Star: Robert Kelker-Kelly (BO BRADY)

the 1994 SOAP OPERA DIGEST AWARDS

Days of Our Lives returned to its full strength, walking away with eleven of the sixteen awards presented. Once again broadcast in primetime, this year's ceremony was co-hosted by Lisa Rinna (BILLIE REED), who won Best Female Newcomer, and *Frasier* star Kelsey Grammer. While accepting her award, Rinna thanked "Fred," a nickname for her boyfriend and future husband Harry Hamlin. Robert Kelker-Kelly won the Outstanding Lead Actor award for playing Bo, a role that had racked up a number of awards for his predecessor, Peter Reckell.

Winners

Outstanding Daytime Soap: *Days of Our Lives*

Outstanding Lead Actor: Robert Kelker-Kelly (BO BRADY)

Outstanding Supporting Actress: Deborah Adair (KATE ROBERTS)

Outstanding Villain/Villainess: Louise Sorel (VIVIAN ALAMAIN)

Outstanding Male Newcomer: Patrick Muldoon (AUSTIN REED)

Outstanding Female Newcomer: Lisa Rinna (BILLIE REED)

Favorite Storyline: "Who Fathered Marlena's Baby?"

Outstanding Musical Achievement: *Days of Our Lives*

Outstanding Child Actor: Scott Groff (SHAWN-DOUGLAS BRADY)

Hottest Male Star: Drake Hogestyn (JOHN BLACK)

Hottest Female Star: Melissa Reeves (JENNIFER HORTON)

the 1995 *SOAP OPERA DIGEST* AWARDS

John Larroquette of *The John Larroquette Show* co-hosted the ceremony joined by an actress from each network; Louise Sorel (VIVIAN ALAMAIN) represented NBC and won the award for Outstanding Female Scene Stealer. Deidre Hall picked up a record-setting fifth award as Best Actress.

Winners

Outstanding Daytime Soap: *Days of Our Lives*

Outstanding Lead Actress: Deidre Hall (DR. MARLENA EVANS)

Hottest Male Star: Drake Hogestyn (JOHN BLACK)

Outstanding Villain: Jason Brooks (PETER BLAKE)

Outstanding Female Scene Stealer: Louise Sorel (VIVIAN ALAMAIN)

Hottest Soap Couple: Robert Kelker-Kelly and Lisa Rinna
(BO BRADY and BILLIE REED)

Louise Sorel (VIVIAN ALAMAIN) has won Soap Opera Digest awards in four categories and has co-hosted the ceremony.

the 1996 *Soap Opera Digest* Awards

This year's awards ceremony aired on Valentine's Day. *Frasier* costar Jane Leeves hosted the show with a soap actor from each network; Drake Hogestyn (JOHN BLACK) represented NBC. Peter Reckell, who had returned to *Days of Our Lives* in the late summer and whose scenes barely made it into the eligibility period, managed to pull down the award for Hottest Male Star. His leading lady, Kristian Alfonso, however, failed to win the Hottest Female Star award.

Winners

Outstanding Daytime Soap: *Days of Our Lives*

Hottest Male Star: Peter Reckell (BO BRADY)

Outstanding Supporting Actress: Louise Sorel (VIVIAN ALAMAIN)

Outstanding Villainess: Alison Sweeney (SAMI BRADY)

Nominees

Hottest Female Star: Kristian Alfonso (HOPE WILLIAMS BRADY)

the 1997 *Soap Opera Digest* Awards

For the first time, the soaps eligible to be named favorite soap were limited to a list of three. While *Days* was nominated, *General Hospital* walked away with the award, along with a third of the acting statuettes. The ceremony was held in the Amphitheater at Universal Studios and was hosted by talk show host (and *Days* fan) Leeza Gibbons along with an actor from each network. Austin Peck (AUSTIN REED), who along with Christie Clark (CARRIE BRADY) picked up an award for Hottest Romance, represented NBC.

Winners

Outstanding Villain: Joseph Mascolo (Stefano DiMera)

Outstanding Female Showstopper: Louise Sorel (Vivian Alamain)

Hottest Romance: Christie Clark and Austin Peck
(CARRIE BRADY and AUSTIN REED)

Nominees
Outstanding Daytime Soap: *Days of Our Lives*

Outstanding Lead Actress: Eileen Davidson (KRISTEN DIMERA)

Hottest Male Star: Drake Hogestyn (JOHN BLACK)

the 1998 SOAP OPERA AWARDS

The award show came close to being cancelled this year when word leaked out that a staff member from *General Hospital* had acquired several hundred issues of *Soap Opera Digest* and used them to vote for their show. When *Days of Our Lives* executive producer Ken Corday found out, he complained to NBC, who threatened to pull the plug on the show until *Soap Opera Digest* offered to do a second ballot. As it turned out, *General Hospital* remained the big winner for the second year in a row. The ceremony was hosted by Leeza Gibbons again as well as Drake Hogestyn (JOHN BLACK), who introduced *Soap Opera Digest* editor Lynn Leahy as the editor of a rival magazine. A highlight of the evening was Eileen Davidson presenting the Hottest Male Star award as her Susan Banks persona.

Winners
Outstanding Villainess: Alison Sweeney (SAMI BRADY)

Outstanding Male Newcomer: Jensen Ackles (ERIC BRADY)

Nominees
Outstanding Lead Actress: Eileen Davidson (KRISTEN BLAKE, SUSAN BANKS, and SISTER MARY MOIRA BANKS)

Outstanding Male Scene Stealer: Ivan G'Vera (IVAN MARAIS)

Hottest Romance: Drake Hogestyn and Deidre Hall
(JOHN BLACK and DR. MARLENA EVANS)

Alison Sweeney (SAMI BRADY) has won a pair of
Soap Opera Digest awards as Best Villainess.

Proposed Spin-offs

SO POPULAR WERE Doug and Julie that the network contemplated spinning them off into their very own soap opera. That idea was killed in the boardroom. The characters were ultimately considered too integral to *Days'* success to lose.

When Mickey Horton was suffering from amnesia and living on a farm with Maggie, NBC toyed with the idea of spinning them off into their own rustic soap opera.

A comic spin-off revolving around the character of Calliope Jones came close to making it onto the air. Among the titles kicked around for the show were *Calliope, Keeping Up with the Joneses,* and *Sunnyside Up.* John de Lancie had been brought back to *Days* with the intention of sending him and Calliope off into the new show together. The spin-off would have taken place in the middle-class neighborhood in Queens, New York, where Calliope grew up. Calliope's relatives would have formed the show's core family. The writers' strike pushed back the show's launch. In the meantime, staff changes took place at the network. Jackie Smith, the new head of daytime programming, decided to shelve the comic *Days* spin-off in favor of the more dramatic and racially integrated *Generations,* which debuted the following year.

Pacific Lives was supposed to be launched to coincide with the show's twenty-fifth anniversary. Ken Corday had worked on the show with former *Days* head writer Pat Falken Smith. The series would have featured members of the Horton family and would have taken place in the Pacific

Rim from Hawaii to Japan. The expense of such an undertaking, much of which would have been taped on location, probably made the series less appealing.

One of the perks that lured Deidre Hall back to *Days* in 1991 was the opportunity to executive produce a series of her own. Soap opera journalists expected this series to be a much talked about *Days* spin-off titled *Manhattan Lives*. As the title implies, the show would have been set in New York City. Hall would have not only executive produced it, she would also have starred. The character of Carrie Brady was also expected to relocate from Salem to New York. Like all the other *Days'* spin-offs that had been proposed through the years, this one never made it to the pilot stage. Some industry insiders have speculated that NBC's increased desire to produce its own soap operas rather than air another soap owned by Corday Productions and Columbia TriStar killed the show.

Manhattan Lives was but the latest in a line of spin-offs contemplated for the character of Marlena Evans. Back when she was involved with Don Craig, the network considered giving them their own show. And again, when Marlena was married to Roman Brady, the network toyed with them headlining a brand new soap.

the 1960s

1. What was Alice Horton's maiden name?

(a) Kelly   (b) Grayson   (c) Cooper   (d) Hoffman

2. For what crime was teenaged Julie Olson arrested in the very first episode?

(a) possession of marijuana   (b) truancy

(c) shoplifting   (d) drunk driving

3. What illness threatened Bill Horton's career as a surgeon?

(a) arthritis   (b) tuberculosis of the bone

(c) Finns-Atkins disorder   (d) a brain tumor

4. What drove Marie Horton into the convent?

(a) She had an abortion.

(b) She accidentally murdered her own child.

(b) She murdered her fiancé during a fight.

(d) She unwittingly fell in love with her own brother.

5. Why did Susan Hunter kill her husband?

(a) She caught him in bed with Julie Olson.

(b) He was trying to rape her.

(c) He caused her miscarriage.

(d) She blamed him for the accidental death of their son.

the 1970s

6. For what crime was Bill Horton sentenced to three years in prison?

(a) raping Laura

(b) the wrongful death of his sister-in-law Kitty

(c) practicing medicine without a license

(d) selling prescriptions

7. What was the name of the roman à clef that Eric Peters wrote?

    (a) *Outside Looking In*   (b) *In My Brother's Shadow*

    (c) *Physician, Heal Thyself*   (d) *Smalltown Sins*

8. What was the name of the sanitarium to which Mickey Horton was committed?

    (a) All Saints   (b) Bayview   (c) The Chadwick Center   (d) Dunn

9. What caused Amanda Howard to break her engagement to Dr. Neil Curtis on the night before their wedding?

    (a) She learned that she was dying from a brain tumor.

    (b) He refused to sign a prenuptial agreement.

    (c) She caught him with a prostitute.

    (d) He missed the rehearsal dinner because he was gambling.

10. Mike Horton married Margo Anderman despite her suffering from what medical condition?

    (a) sterility   (b) a weak heart   (c) leukemia   (d) a brain tumor

the 1980s

11. Who was Jessica Blake's biological father?

    (a) Don Craig   (b) Neil Curtis

    (c) Kellam Chandler   (d) Alex Marshall

12. Why did Liz Curtis shoot Marie Horton?

    (a) An enraged Marie Horton had pulled a knife on Liz.

    (b) Liz mistook Marie for a prowler.

    (c) Liz was aiming for Stefano and shot Marie by mistake.

    (d) Stefano DiMera had brainwashed Liz to kill Marie.

13. To what gang did Pete Jannings once belong?

    (a) The Razors   (b) The Vipers

    (c) The Reapers   (d) The Front Street Gang

14. Where did Patch and Kayla honeymoon the first time they got married?

(a) Canada   (b) New York City

(c) in the Orient   (d) right in Salem

15. What did Nick Corelli rename the nightclub Blondie's?

(a) Wings   (b) Nick's Place   (c) Eve's Garden   (d) Shenanigans

the 1990s

16. What was the name of the newspaper that Jack Deveraux once owned?

(a) *The Guardian*   (b) *The Spectator*

(c) *The Herald*   (d) *The Banner*

17. Which of Roman Brady's family members, while suffering from a multiple personality disorder, shot him in the head?

(a) his brother Bo   (b) his sister Kimberly

(c) his daughter Sami   (d) his mother Caroline

18. What scarred Carrie Brady's face on the same night she was named "The Face of the '90s" by *Bella* magazine?

(a) A jealous Sami pushed her through a window.

(b) A mobster threw acid in her face.

(c) A chandelier fell on top of her.

(d) She fell down an elevator shaft.

19. Which murdered villain was released from Hell to help Satan reclaim Marlena Evans?

(a) Kellam Chandler   (b) Harper Deveraux

(c) Curtis Reed   (d) Stella Lombard

20. In which part of Vivian Alamain's anatomy did Stefano DiMera have a mood-altering microchip implanted?

(a) earlobe   (b) tooth   (c) left hand   (d) the base of her skull

No More Multiple Choice

21. Fill in the blanks in the Horton family tree to connect Alice with great-great-grandson Scott Banning.

Alice Horton

_____

_____

_____

Scott Banning

22. Name three other identities, in order, that John Black has had.

_____

_____

_____

23. Name the four *Days of Our Lives* performers who have co-hosted the Daytime Emmy Awards.

_____

_____

_____

_____

24. Name Stefano DiMera's six biological children and signify whether each is living or dead.

_____DEAD/ALIVE

_____DEAD/ALIVE

_____DEAD/ALIVE

_____DEAD/ALIVE

_____DEAD/ALIVE

_____DEAD/ALIVE

25. Name all four Banks quadruplets.

_____

_____

_____

_____

Cast List

alphabetical by performer's last name

James Acheson	JACK DEVERAUX (1987)
Jensen Ackles	ERIC BRADY (1997–present)
Deborah Adair	KATE ROBERTS KIRIAKIS (1993–95)
Joseph Adams	JACK DEVERAUX (1987)
Wesley Addy	DR. COOPER (1966–67)
Antony Alda	JOHNNY CORELLI (1990–91)
Robert Alda	DR. STUART WHYLAND (1981)
Sarah Aldrich	JILL STEVENS (1996–97)
Rhonda Aldrick	KAYLA BRADY (1989)
Denise Alexander	SUSAN HUNTER MARTIN (1966–73)
Victor Alfieri	FRANCO KELLY (1996–98)
Kristian Alfonso	HOPE WILLIAMS WELCH BRADY (1983–87, 1990, 1994–present)
Jed Allan	DON CRAIG (1971–85)
Jeremy Allen	JEREMY JACOBS (1989)
Krista Allen-Moritt	BILLIE REED BRADY (1996–present)
John Amour	DR. MIKE HORTON (1971–73)
Deke Anderson	EDDIE REED (1989)

Bill Andes	HARLEY MARSHALL (1979–80)
Brian Andrews	DR. MIKE HORTON (1970)
Christian Andrews	BUD (1987–90)
Tina Andrews	VALERIE GRANT (1975–77)
John Aniston	DR. ERIC RICHARDS (1969–70) and VICTOR KIRIAKIS (1985–97)
Frank Annese	BARRY REID (1984–85)
Jay Anthony	ERNESTO (1998)
Christina Applegate	BURT GRIZZELL (1972)
Ben Archibek	DR. NEIL CURTIS (1973)
Vaughn Armstrong	DAVID CALDWELL (1994)
Ronit Arnoff	SAMI BRADY (1984)
Adrian Arnold	MAX BRADY (1987)
Rod Arrants	RICHARD CATES (1985–86)
Matthew Ashford	JACK DEVERAUX (1987–93)
Frank Ashmore	BRENT CAVANAUGH (1981)
Brian Autenrieth	ZACH PARKER (1984–85)
Joel Bailey	CAMERON DAVIS (1985–86)
Andrea Barber	CARRIE BRADY (1982–86)
Ron Barker	CHIEF TARRINGTON (1988–92)
Julian Barnes	ANDREW DONOVAN (1988) and DR. GODDARD (1992)
Eileen Barnett	BROOKE HAMILTON (aka STEPHANIE WOODRUFF) (1978–80)
Sharon Barr	BILLIE (1983–84)
Patricia Barry	ADDIE HORTON OLSON WILLIAMS (1971–74)
Chad Barstad	DAVID BANNING (1967–70)
Dan Barton	EARL ROSCOE (1979–80)
William H. Bassett	DR. WALTER GRIFFIN (1977–78)
Charles Bateman	MAXWELL JARVIS (1980–81)

Matt Battaglia	J. L. KING (1997)
Jaime Lyn Bauer	DR. LAURA SPENCER HORTON (1993–present)
Melissa Baum	CASSIE SCOFIELD (1990–91)
Michael Bays	JULIO RAMÍREZ (1988–89)
Brigid Bazlen	MARY ANDERSON (1972)
Terrence Beasor	JONATHAN RUTHERFORD (1985) and ERNESTO TOSCANO (1989)
Rory Beauregard	ERIC BRADY (1984)
Jim Beaver	FATHER TIMOTHY JANSEN (1996–97)
Barbara Beckley	CAROLINE BRADY (1984–85)
Fred Beir	LARRY ATWOOD (1977–78)
Felecia M. Bell	GLYNNIS TURNER (1990–91)
Nick Benedict	CURTIS REED (1993–95, 1997)
Brenda Benet	LEE DUMONDE (1979–82)
Oscar Beregi Jr.	SERGIO (1970, 1972)
Richard Bergman	BRETT FREDERICKS (1983)
Jason Bernard	PRESTON WADE (1982)
Richard Biggs	DR. MARCUS HUNTER (1987–92)
Dick Billingsley	SCOTTY BANNING (1981–83)
Barry Blakeley	JERRY RINEHART (1978–79)
Vasili Bogazianos	OZZIE (1993)
Craig Bond	DR. MIKE HORTON (1969)
Carla Borelli	MARY ANDERSON (1975)
Joseph Bottoms	CAL WINTERS (1991)
Pamela Bowen	LESLIE LANDAMAN (1986–87)
Tanya Boyd	CELESTE PERRAULT (aka FRANKIE BROOKS) (1994–present)
Tracey E. Bregman	DONNA TEMPLE CRAIG (1978–80)
Ryan Brennan	MAX BRADY (1987–88, 1990–92)
Angelica Bridges	SHARON TAYLOR (1996)

Don Briscoe	TONY MERRITT (1966)
Danielle Brisebois	SASHA ROBERTS (1987)
Stanley Brock	HOWIE HOFFSTEDDER (1983–86)
Elaine Bromka	STELLA LOMBARD (1992)
Fritz Bronner	STEVEN MILLER (1993)
Aimee Brooks	SARAH HORTON (1990)
J. Cynthia Brooks	TAYLOR MCCALL (1992–93)
Jason Brooks	PETER BLAKE (1993–96, 1997–98)
Randy Brooks	DESMOND (1988)
Stephen Brooks	JOSHUA FALLON (1980–81)
Shellye Broughton	LEXIE BROOKS CARVER (1993)
Lew Brown	SHAWN BRADY (1984–85)
Peter Brown	DR. GREG PETERS (1972–79)
Roger Aaron Brown	DANNY GRANT (1981–85)
Tom Brown	NATHAN CURTIS (1975–76)
Robert Brubaker	JOHN MARTIN (1966–71)
Pamela Brull	ELLEN HAWK (1988)
Perry Bullington	BRENT CAVANAUGH (1980–81)
Brooke Bundy	REBECCA NORTH LECLAIR (1975–77)
Lauren Ann Bundy	SAMI BRADY (1985)
Richard Burgi	PHILIP COLLIER (1992–93)
Elizabeth Burr	BARBARA STEWART (1986–87)
Steve Burton	HARRIS MICHAELS (1988)
Ruth Buzzi	LETICIA BRADFORD (1983)
Lorenzo Caccialanza	NICO (1988–91)
Adam Caine	EDMUND (1998)
Bill Cakmis	YURI (1986)
John Callahan	ARTIE DOYLE (1989) and TYLER MALONE (1983)
John Calvin	ARTHUR DOWNEY (1989–90)

Stephanie Cameron	JENNIFER HORTON DEVERAUX (1995–98)
Joseph Campanella	HARPER DEVERAUX (1987–88, 1990–92)
Sandra Canning	GRACE JEFFRIES (1989–90)
Macdonald Carey	DR. TOM HORTON SR. (1965–94)
Karen Carlson	SHEILA HAMMOND (1971)
Paul Carr	DR. BILL HORTON (1965–66)
Bob Carraway	SCOTT BANNING (1968)
Dee Carroll	ADELE WINSTON HAMILTON (1975–76)
Jody Carter	CAROLINE BRADY (1984)
Lane Caudell	WOODY KING (1982–83)
Alina Cenal	CARMEN (1995, 1996, 1997)
Patrice Chanel	GAIL CARSON (1989) and JOAN HUNT (1998)
Judith Chapman	ANJELICA DEVERAUX CURTIS (1989–90)
Crystal Chappell	DR. CARLY MANNING KIRIAKIS (aka KATERINA VON LEUSCHNER) (1990–93)
Ariana Chase	KIMBERLY BRADY (1993)
Maree Cheatham	MARIE HORTON MERRITT CURTIS (1965–68, 1970–73, 1994, 1996)
Dick Christie	STANLEY KRAKOWSKI (1990)
Eric Christmas	FATHER FRANCIS (1995, 1996)
Charles Cioffi	ERNESTO TOSCANO (1990)
Christie Clark	CARRIE BRADY REED (1986–90, 1992–present)
Lynn Clark	MADELINE ARMSTRONG (1990–92)
John Clarke	MICKEY HORTON (1965–present)
Mindy Clarke	FAITH TAYLOR (1989–90)
Robert Clary	ROBERT LECLAIR (1972–73, 1975–80, 1981–83, 1986)
Clive Clerk	DAVID MARTIN (1966–67)
Brian Cole	DEREK SWEENEY (1986–87)
Jack Coleman	JAKE KOSITCHEK (1981–82)

Douglas Coler	DR. PICCARD (1996)
Richard A. Colla	TONY MERRITT (1965–66)
Joe Colligan	ETHAN REILLY (1987–88)
Jolina Collins	JASMINE (1984–85)
Scott Colomby	JOSÉ TORRES (1988)
Corinne Conley	PHYLLIS ANDERSON CURTIS (1973–82)
Cathy Connell	BARBARA NEWIRTH (1992)
Lawrence Cook	PAUL GRANT (1975–76)
Paul Coufos	DR. MIKE HORTON (1981–82)
Doug Cox	BOB RUSH (1990)
Barbara Crampton	TRISTA EVANS BRADFORD (1983)
Roark Critchlow	DR. MIKE HORTON (1994–present)
Denise Crosby	LISA DAVIS (1980)
Rusty Cundieff	THEO CARVER (1985)
Sonia Curtis	NANCY (1986)
Barry Cutler	LOGAN MICHAELS, THE PARROT MAN (1995–96)
Deborah Dalton	CASSIE BURNS (1980–81)
Cathy Daly	CATHY BRETON (1979–80)
Michael Dante	BARNEY JANNINGS (1984)
Patrika Darbo	NANCY WESLEY (1998–present)
Bryan Dattilo	LUCAS ROBERTS (1993–present)
Marty Davich	MARTY (1977–93)
Eileen Davidson	KRISTEN BLAKE DIMERA (1993–98), SUSAN BANKS (1996–98), SISTER MARY MOIRA BANKS (1997–98), THOMAS BANKS (1997), and PENELOPE KENT (1998)
Lane Davies	DR. EVAN WHYLAND (1981–82)
Floy Dean	DR. LAURA SPENCER HORTON (1966)
Alan Decker	DR. MIKE HORTON (1970–71)
Dick De Coit	DR. MIKE HORTON (1973)

Roger De Koven	DR. JAMES SPENCER (1968–69)
John de Lancie	EUGENE BRADFORD (1982–86, 1989)
Larry Delaney	JAY LIVINGSTON (1973–74, 1976, 1979)
Pat Delaney	RACHEL BLAKE (1995–96)
George Deloy	ORPHEUS (1986–87)
Jack Denbo	JACK CLAYTON (1974–77)
Francis De Sales	DR. JAMES SPENCER (1971)
Don Diamont	CARLO FORENZA (1984–85)
Susan Diol	EMMY BORDEN (1990–91)
Ben DiTosti	BEN, THE PIANO PLAYER (1974–77, 1980)
Carla Doherty	JULIE OLSON (1965–66)
Michael Dorn	JIMMY (1986–87)
Steve Doubet	DAVID BANNING (1975)
Burt Douglas	JIM FISK (1965) and SAM MONROE (1974–75)
Diana Douglas	MARTHA EVANS (1977–79)
Harrison Douglas	IAN GRIFFITH (1985)
Frederick Downs	HANK (1973–80)
Mark Drexler	ROGER LOMBARD (1992)
Doug Dudley	TED MCMANNIS (1978–79)
Kathy Dunn	JULIE OLSON (1967)
Marj Dusay	VIVIAN ALAMAIN (1993)
Steve Eastin	COLONEL ALFRED JERICHO (1989–90)
Joyce Easton	JANET BANNING (1967–68)
Michael Easton	TANNER SCOFIELD (1990–92)
Bobby Eilbacher	DR. MIKE HORTON (1970)
Jane Elliot	ANJELICA DEVERAUX CURTIS (1987–89)
Katherine Ellis	TAYLOR WALKER (1998–present)
Karen Ericson	NORA BASSETT (1979)
Rob Estes	GLENN GALLAGHER (1986–87)
Wesley Eure	DR. MIKE HORTON (1974–81)

Judi Evans	ADRIENNE JOHNSON KIRIAKIS (1986–91)
Mary Beth Evans	KAYLA BRADY JOHNSON (1986–92)
Mike Farrell	SCOTT BANNING (1968–70)
Frank Fata	STEFANO DIMERA (1991)
Melinda O. Fee	MARY ANDERSON MARSHALL (1981–82)
Catherine Ferrar	JULIE OLSON (1967–68)
Chip Fields	TONI JOHNSON (1978–79)
Cindy Fisher	DIANE PARKER (1984)
Susan Flannery	DR. LAURA SPENCER HORTON (1966–75)
Rose Fonseca	VALERIE GRANT (1977–78)
Lois Foraker	SIMONE BERTE (1996)
Michael Forest	CORLEY MAXWELL (1979–80)
Rosemary Forsyth	DR. LAURA SPENCER HORTON (1976–80)
Don Frabotta	DAVE (1973–93)
Angelique Francis	LEXIE BROOKS CARVER (1989–90, 1992)
Genie Francis	DIANA COLVILLE (1987–89)
Mary Frann	AMANDA HOWARD PETERS (1974–79)
Helen Funai	KIM DOUGLAS (1971–72, 1976–77)
Loretta Fury	AMELIA CRAIG (1978–79)
Ivan G'Vera	HENRI VON LEUSCHNER (1990) and IVAN MARAIS (1991–present)
Holly Gagnier	IVY SELEJKO JANNINGS (1984–86)
Joseph Gallison	DR. NEIL CURTIS (1974–91)
Winnie Gardner	DAISY HAWKINS (1983)
Joy Garrett	JOSEPHINE "JO" JOHNSON (1987–93)
Bennye Gatteys	SUSAN HUNTER MARTIN PETERS (1973–76)
Martha Gehman	MICHELLE BERNARD (1996)
Kirk Geiger	CHAD WEBSTER (1990)
Robert Gentry	DR. RICHARD HUNT (1994–95)
Carrie Genzel	ALI MCINTYRE, R.N. (1997–98)

Gerry Gibson	SIMMONS (1986–92)
Livia Ginise	MITZI RUMMLEY MATUSO (1982–83)
Richard Gittings	BOB ANDERSON (1978)
Regina Gleason	KITTY HORTON (1967–69)
Terence O. Goodman	SERGEANT MCBRIDE (1984–85)
Jennifer Goodwin	DOREEN (1998)
Cyndi James Gossett	LEXIE BROOKS (1988–89)
Coleen Gray	DIANE HUNTER (1967–68)
Staci Greason	ISABELLA TOSCANO BLACK (1989–92, 1995)
Brian Lane Green	ALAN BRAND (1987–89)
Kaela Green	EMILY (1995)
Kim Morgan Greene	SHEILA SALSBURY (aka KELLY PARKER) (1990)
Jeff Griggs	JUDE ST. CLAIR (1995–96)
Scott Groff	SHAWN-DOUGLAS BRADY (1990–95)
Vincent Guastaferro	MARK (1995)
Richard Guthrie	DAVID BANNING (1975–81)
Deidre Hall	DR. MARLENA EVANS CRAIG BRADY (1976–87, 1991–present)
Andrea Hall-Lovell	SAMANTHA EVANS (1977–80, 1982)
Tom Hallick	MAXWELL HATHAWAY (1984)
Lori Hallier	YVETTE DUPRES (1989–90)
Bradley Hallock	ERIC BRADY (1986–92)
Ann Hamilton	RACHEL BLAKE (1995–96)
Randy Hamilton	RON WYCHE (1986–88)
James Hampton	SAUL TAYLOR (1989)
Robert Hanley	ERIC BRADY (1992)
Thomas Havens	STAN KOSITCHEK (1979)
Jerry Hawkins	FRED HARRIS (1993–94)
Bill Hayes	DOUG WILLIAMS (aka BRENT DOUGLAS) (1970–84, 1986–87, 1993, 1994–95, 1996) and BYRON CARMICHAEL (1979)

Susan Seaforth Hayes	JULIE OLSON WILLIAMS (1968–84, 1990–96)
Rick Hearst	SCOTTY BANNING (1989–90)
Wayne Heffley	VERN SCOFIELD (1988–93)
Elaine Hendrix	BRANDEE (1993)
Stephen Anthony Henry	LUKE (1986–88)
Lynn Herring	LISANNE GARDNER (1992)
Doris Hess	COOK (1996)
Darby Hinton	IAN GRIFFITH (1985–86)
Deborah Hobart	MOLLY CHASE (1984) and JILL BAILEY (1990–91)
Robert Hogan	SCOTT BANNING (1970–71)
Drake Hogestyn	JOHN BLACK (aka ROMAN BRADY, FORREST ALAMAIN, and JOHN STEVENS) (1986–present)
Victor Holchak	JIM PHILLIPS (1971, 1974–75)
Wade Holdsworth	DR. MIKE HORTON (1969)
Fred Holliday	RON WYCHE (1988–91)
James Hong	COLONEL CHENGSU (1967–68) and BABA SOO LAN (1985)
Patricia Hornung	JANENE WHITNEY (1969–70)
Anne Marie Howard	KIMBERLY BRADY (1990–91)
John Howard	CLIFF PATTERSON (1971)
Lisa Howard	APRIL RAMIREZ (1988–91)
Jean Howell	MARY MCCALL (1967)
Bill Hufsey	EMILIO RAMIREZ (1988–90)
Craig Hundley	TIMMY MCCALL (1967)
Leann Hunley	ANNA DIMERA (1982–86)
Sherry Hursey	PAULA CARSON (1988–89)
Hettie Lynne Hurtes	TRACY NORTH (1979) and RADIO ANNOUNCER (1997)
Ron Husmann	TONY MERRITT (1966–67)

Patricia Huston	ADDIE HORTON OLSON (1965–66)
Barrie Ingham	LEOPOLD BRONSKI (1985)
Paul Henry Itkin	JOHNNY COLLINS (1975–77)
Stan Ivar	DANIEL SCOTT (1994–96)
Mark Jacobs	ARTIE BERGEN (1977–79)
Billy Jayne	VITO (1987)
George Jenesky	NICK CORELLI (1981, 1984, 1986–90)
Julie Jeter	SASHA ROBERTS (1986)
Kenneth Jezek	LARS ENGLUND (1986–87)
Gail Johnson	MIMI GROSSET (1979–80)
Renée Jones	NIKKI WADE (1982–83) and LEXIE BROOKS CARVER (1993–present)
James Carroll Jordan	STEVEN OLSON (1972)
S. Marc Jordan	ELI JACOBS (1986–87, 1989)
Bill Joyce	KELLAM CHANDLER (1980–81)
Stanley Kamel	ERIC PETERS (1972–76)
Valerie Karasek	SERENA COLVILLE (1987–88)
Jane Kean	DIANE HUNTER (1965–66)
Noah Keen	RAY STONE (1979)
Paul Keenan	TODD CHANDLER (1980–81)
William Keene	DR. LUBICK (1973–76)
Elizabeth Keifer	AMY COOPER (1985)
Robert Kelker-Kelly	BO BRADY (1992–95)
Susan Keller	MARY ANDERSON MARSHALL (1980)
Lisa Robin Kelly	JILL STEVENS (1996)
Sally Kemp	NORA BASSETT (1983)
Paul Kersey	ALAN HARRIS (1993–95)
Lee Kessler	ANNE GOLDBERG (1993–94)
Paige Kettner	ABIGAIL JOANNA DEVERAUX (1994–98)
Ryanne Kettner	ABIGAIL JOANNA DEVERAUX (1994–98)

Dana Kimmell	DIANE PARKER (1983–84)
Meegan King	PETE CURTIS (1978–79)
Robert Knapp	BEN OLSON (1965)
Tracy Kolis	REBECCA DOWNEY (1989–90)
Yvonna Kopacz	WENDY REARDON (1996–97)
Lauren Koslow	KATE ROBERTS KIRIAKIS (1996–present)
Wortham Krimmer	CAL WINTERS (1989–90)
Ron Kuhlman	JIMMY PORTERFIELD (1984–85) and HANK TOBIN (1989)
Wallace Kurth	JUSTIN KIRIAKIS (1987–91)
Hilary Labow	FELICITY YORK (1985)
Rene Lamart	JAKE KOSITCHEK (1981)
Clayton Landey	GREGORY (1990–92)
Shana Lane-Block	SARAH HORTON (1989)
Adrienne Larussa	BROOKE HAMILTON (1975–77)
Harry Lauter	CRAIG MERRITT (1966)
John Lavachielli	HANK TOBIN (1989)
Ron Leath	HENDERSON (1987–present)
Stuart Lee	DR. MIKE HORTON (1973)
Beverly Leech	BIANCA TORRES (1988)
Roberta Leighton	GINGER DAWSON (1991–92)
Michael Leon	PETE JANNINGS (1983–86)
Ketty Lester	HELEN GRANT (1975–77)
Thyme Lewis	JONAH CARVER (1993–97)
Gloria Loring	LIZ CHANDLER CURTIS (1980–86)
Charles Lucia	HART BENNETT (1985)
Judi Evans Luciano	ADRIENNE JOHNSON KIRIAKIS (1986–91)
William Lucking	HARRY CHANEY (1981)
James Luisi	DUKE JOHNSON (1987, 1990–92) and EARL JOHNSON (1989)

John Lupton	DR. TOMMY HORTON JR. (aka DR. MARK BROOKS) (1967–72, 1975–79)
Charles Macaulay	DR. ELLIOT KINCAID (1967–68)
Ryan MacDonald	SCOTT BANNING (1971–73)
Peter MacLean	DR. PAUL WHITMAN (1977)
Catherine MacNeal	PAT HAMILTON (1993–95, 1997)
Elizabeth MacRae	PHYLLIS ANDERSON (1977)
Robert Mailhouse	BRIAN SCOFIELD (1990–92)
Edward Mallory	DR. BILL HORTON (1966–80, 1991–92)
Christian Malmin	JAY (1998–present)
Robert Mandan	JONSEY JONES (1997–98)
Gloria Manners	CARRIE SPENCER (1971, 1975, 1979)
Flip Mark	STEVEN OLSON (1965)
Scott Marlowe	ERIC BRADY (1984)
Anne-Marie Martin	GWEN DAVIES (1982–85)
John Martin	ROBERT BRENNAN (1985)
Mikey Martin	DOUGIE LECLAIR (1979–80)
Gregg Marx	DAVID BANNING (1981–83)
Joseph Mascolo	DR. TUTANO (1968) and STEFANO DiMERA (1982–85, 1988, 1993–present)
Eric Mason	ERNESTO TOSCANO (1990)
Margaret Mason	LINDA PATTERSON PHILLIPS ANDERSON (1970–71, 1975–80, 1982)
Andrew Massett	LARRY WELCH (1983–85)
Braden Matthews	TRAVIS MALLOY (1997)
Brian Matthews	BROTHER MARTIN (1985–86)
John Matthews	DR. ELLIOT KINCAID (1968)
Monet Mazur	BRANDEE (1993)
Michael McCay	BONKERS (1997)

Peggy McCay	CAROLINE BRADY (1982, 1985–present)
Marilyn McCoo	TAMARA PRICE (1986–87)
George McDaniel	DR. JORDAN BARR (1979–80)
Kristi McDaniel	SARAH (1995–96)
Marilyn McIntyre	JO JOHNSON (1993)
David McLean	CRAIG MERRITT (1965–67)
Frank McLean	SHAWN BRADY (1989–90)
Catherine McLeod	CLAIRE LARKIN (1968–69)
Sandy McPeak	ORION HAWK (1988)
Corinne Michaels	JOANNE BARNES (1979–80)
Tracy Middendorf	CARRIE BRADY REED (1990–92)
Kelley Miles	DANA (1981–83)
Gary Miller	HOGAN (1987–88)
Eric Mills	MATT (1985–86)
Stephen Mines	DAVID MARTIN (1966)
Dani Minnick	REBECCA MORRISON (1992–93)
Muriel Minot	MARJORIE RUTHERFORD (1985)
Karen Moncrieff	GABRIELLE PASCAL (1987–88)
Belinda Montgomery	SYLVIE GALLAGHER (1986–87)
Deborah Moore	DANIELLE STEVENS (1991–92)
Rob Moran	T. C. GREER (1997)
Camilla More	JANICE KENNEDY (1985), GILLIAN FORRESTER (1986–87), and GRACE FORRESTER (1987–88)
Carey More	GRACE FORRESTER (1987)
Shelley Taylor Morgan	ANJELICA DEVERAUX CURTIS (1989)
Julianne Morris	GRETA (aka SWAMP GIRL) (1998–present)
Gregory Mortensen	PAUL STEWART (1986)
Ronn Moss	WAITER (1984)
Patrick Muldoon	AUSTIN REED (1992–95)
Yvette Napier	SASHA ROBERTS (1987)

Christopher Neame	OGDEN VAUGHN (aka DR. VERTIGO) (1986)
Herbert Nelson	PHIL PETERS (1972–75)
Arthel Neville	SANDRA (1993)
Michelle Nicastro	SASHA ROBERTS (1987)
Stephen Nichols	STEVE "PATCH" JOHNSON (1985–90)
Martha Nix	JANICE BARNES (1976–77)
Chelsea Noble	KRISTINA ANDROPOLUS (1988)
Heather North	SANDY HORTON (1967–71)
Wayne Northrop	ROMAN BRADY (1981–84, 1991–94)
Collin O'Donnell	SHAWN DOUGLAS BRADY (1995–present)
Michael O'Neill	FATHER TIMOTHY JANSEN (1994–95)
Terry O'Sullivan	RICHARD HUNTER (1966–68)
Susan Oliver	DR. LAURA SPENCER HORTON (1975–76)
Kristina Osterhaut	HOPE WILLIAMS BRADY (1974)
Scott Palmer	JOSHUA FALLON (1981–82)
Frank Parker	SHAWN BRADY (1983–84, 1985–89, 1990–present)
Catherine Parks	MITZI RUMMLEY MATUSO (1982)
Miriam Parrish	JAMIE CALDWELL (1993–96)
Nancy Parsons	NURSE JACKSON (1993–94) and MARY BROOK (1996)
Robert Parucha	EDDIE REED (1988–89)
Patsy Pease	KIMBERLY BRADY (1984–94, 1996–present)
Anthony Peck	PORTER ROLLINS (1990)
Austin Peck	AUSTIN REED (1995–present)
J. Eddie Peck	HAWK HAWKINS (1991–92)
Thaao Penghlis	TONY DIMERA (1981–86, 1993–96) and ANDRÉ DIMERA (1983–84)
Christopher Pennock	JOE TAYLOR (1978)
Jennifer Petersen	JENNIFER HORTON (1977–78)

Eric Peterson	SCOTTY BANNING (1978–80)
Gene Peterson	PETER LARKIN (1968–70)
Bradley Pierce	ANDREW DONOVAN (1990–91)
Stack Pierce	KENNY (1977)
Alicia Pillatzke	JEANNIE DONOVAN (1991–92)
Emily Pillatzke	JEANNIE DONOVAN (1991–92)
Phillip Pine	DR. ELLIOT KINCAID (1967)
Judy Pioli	GUINEVERE RUTHERFORD (1985)
Robin Pohle	AMY KOSITCHEK (1978–79)
Larry Poindexter	BEN WELCH (1984)
Rick Porter	HANK TOBIN (1989–90)
Randy Powell	TYLER MALONE (1983)
Ed Prentiss	JOHN MARTIN (1966) and ALEX MARSHALL (1971–72)
Dan Priest	EARL ROSCOE (1978)
Elaine Princi	LINDA ANDERSON (1984–85)
Kyle Puerner	DR. MIKE HORTON (1968–69)
Karen Purcill	DALE GRIFFITH (1985)
Patrick Neil Quinn	RENFRO (1989)
Cassidy Rae	KAREN (1993)
Ford Rainey	FRANK EVANS (1977–78)
Anne Randall	SHEILA HAMMOND (1971–72)
Edward Rayden	DR. MIKE HORTON (1970)
Elsa Rayen	LUCILLE, THE MAID (1998–present)
Richard Raynesford	RENÉ DUMONT (1996)
Marie-Alise Recasner	LYNN BURKE (1994–present)
Peter Reckell	BO BRADY (1983–87, 1990–91, 1995–present)
Quinn Redeker	ALEX MARSHALL (1979–87)
Melissa Reeves	JENNIFER HORTON DEVERAUX (1985–95)
Scott Reeves	JAKE HOGANSEN (1988)

Frances Reid	ALICE GRAYSON HORTON (1965–present)
Tara Reid	ASHLEY (1995)
Deborah Rennard	DR. WHITNEY BAKER (1991)
Alejandro Rey	KARL DUVAL (1976–77)
James Reynolds	ABE CARVER (1981–90, 1991–present)
Tony Rhoades	JESSE LOMBARD (1992)
Michael Rhoton	MAX BRADY (1986–87)
Madlyn Rhue	DAPHNE DIMERA (1982–84)
Hal Riddle	MAX, THE WAITER (1971–75)
Sue Rihr	MADELINE RUTHERFORD BRADFORD (1985)
Lisa Rinna	BILLIE REED (1992–95)
DeAnna Robbins	DIANE PARKER (1984)
Andrew Robinson	COUSIN YURI (1996)
Bumper Robinson	JONAH CARVER (1987–89)
Jay Robinson	MONTY DOLAN (1988–89)
Maurice Roëves	DAVE HALPERN (1986)
Ed Rogers	ED SIMPSON (1979)
Suzanne Rogers	MAGGIE HORTON (1974–present)
Gyl Roland	SHEILA HAMMOND (1972)
Robert Romanus	SPEED SELEJKO (1983–85)
Tom Rosqui	DR. RALPH JANNINGS (1984)
Charlotte Ross	EVE DONOVAN (1987–91)
Pamela Roylance	DR. SANDY HORTON (1983–84)
Reed Rudy	MAX (1997, 1998)
Derya Ruggles	DR. ROBIN JACOBS (1985–87, 1989)
Sky Rumph	ANDREW DONOVAN (1989) and JOEY (1996)
David Ruprecht	DAN RYAN (1990–92)
Al Ruscio	SEÑOR MIGUEL TORRES (1988)
John Russon	DOUGIE LECLAIR (1977)
Natasha Ryan	HOPE WILLIAMS BRADY (1975–80)

Michael Sabatino	LAWRENCE ALAMAIN (1990–93)
Marcella Saint-Amant	DANIELLE FORENZA (1984–85)
Pat Sajak	KEVIN HATHAWAY (1983)
Susan Saldivar	KRISTINA ANDROPOLUS (1988)
Philece Sampler	RENÉE DUMONDE (1980–84)
Ken Sansone	DR. POWELL (1976)
Lanna Saunders	MARIE HORTON (1979–85)
Pamela Saunders	DR. WHITNEY BAKER (1990)
Eric Schiff	KEVIN CATES (1985–86)
Sharon Schlarth	DARLENE JARVIS (1994)
Stephen Schnetzer	STEVEN OLSON (1978–80)
Jeremy Schoenberg	JOHNNY (1982)
Frank Schofield	FRANK EVANS (1979–80)
Avery Schreiber	LEOPOLD ALAMAIN (1990)
Anna Scott	MARIE-HELENE FORTIER (1992)
Camilla Scott	MELISSA ANDERSON (1990–91)
Jean Bruce Scott	JESSICA BLAKE (1980–82)
Bluejean Seacrist	HOPE WILLIAMS BRADY (1997)
Susan Seaforth Hayes	JULIE OLSON WILLIAMS (1968–84, 1990–96)
Jocelyn Seagrave	TANYA HAMPSTEAD (1994)
Hazzan Shaheed	DANNY GRANT (1976)
Charles Shaughnessy	SHANE DONOVAN (1984–92) and DREW DONOVAN (1988)
Eric Sinclair	DURAND (1979)
Nancy Sloan	SALLY (1989)
Martha Smith	DR. SANDY HORTON (1982)
Michael Dwight Smith	DANNY GRANT (1975–78)
Diane Sommerfield	DR. VALERIE GRANT (1981–82)
Louise Sorel	VIVIAN ALAMAIN (1992–present)
Arleen Sorkin	CALLIOPE JONES BRADFORD (1984–90, 1992)

Kevin Spirtas	DR. CRAIG WESLEY (1997–present)
Barbara Stanger	MARY ANDERSON MARSHALL (1975–81)
Sally Stark	SHARON DUVAL (1976–77)
Nancy Stephens	MARY ANDERSON (1975)
John Stephenson	TERRY GILBERT (1979–80)
Maren Stephenson	JENNIFER HORTON (1976–77)
Ashleigh Sterling	SAMI BRADY (1986–90)
K. T. Stevens	HELEN MARTIN (1966–67, 1969)
Kaye Stevens	JERI CLAYTON (1974–79)
Shawn Stevens	OLIVER MARTIN (1982–83)
Benjamin Stewart	EAMES (1981)
Budd Stewart	DICKIE MARTIN (1967)
Catherine Mary Stewart	KAYLA BRADY (1982–83)
Amy Stock-Poynton	BRITTA ENGLUND (1986–87)
Henry Stolow	HANS INVOLT
Christopher Stone	DR. BILL HORTON (1987–88, 1994)
Elizabeth Storm	JANICE BARNES (1987–88)
Ray Stricklyn	HOWARD ALSTON HAWKINS II (1991–92)
Vicki Stuart	VIOLET (1998)
Shannon Sturges	MOLLY BRINKER (1991–92)
Alison Sweeney	SAMI BRADY (1992–present)
Mark Tapscott	BOB ANDERSON (1972–80)
April Tatro	LAVERNE (1998)
Josh Taylor	CHRIS KOSITCHEK (1977–87) and ROMAN BRADY (1997–present)
Tammy Taylor	HOPE WILLIAMS BRADY (1981)
Marshall R. Teague	LEONARD STACY (1984)
Paul Tinder	PAUL STEWART (1987)
Robert Torti	CHARLES VAN DIETER (1993)
Tammy Townsend	WENDY REARDON (1994–96)

William Traylor	JAMES STANHOPE (1976–77)
Lawrence Trimble	THE DRAGON (1985)
Lisa Trusel	MELISSA ANDERSON JANNINGS (1982–88, 1994, 1996)
Nadyne Turney	LINDA PATTERSON (1970)
Shannon Tweed	SAVANNAH WILDER (1985–86)
Hunter Tylo	MARINA TOSCANO JOHNSON (1989–90)
Darrell Thomas Utley	BENJI DIMERA (1988–89, 1990)
Mark Valley	JACK DEVERAUX (1994–97)
Joan Van Ark	JANENE WHITNEY (1970)
Charles Van Eman	TRENT BECKER (1987)
Erik von Detten	NICHOLAS ALAMAIN (1992–93)
Lark Voorhies	WENDY REARDON (1993–94)
Christina Wagoner	SAMI BRADY (1990–92)
Gregory Wagrowski	JAKE SELLERS (1985–86)
David Wallace	TODD CHANDLER (1985–86)
Billy Warlock	FRANKIE BRADY (aka FRANÇOIS VON LEUSCHNER) (1986–88, 1990–91)
Astrid Warner	SANDY HORTON (1967)
Mike Warren	JERRY DAVIS (1976)
Patty Weaver	TRISH CLAYTON BANNING (1974–82)
Kimberly Joy Weber	HOPE WILLIAMS BRADY (1975)
Michael T. Weiss	DR. MIKE HORTON (1985–90)
Jack Wells	DESMOND TOWNS (1979)
Robert Wexler	LESTER HALL (1979–80)
Joseph Whipp	LOU (1995–96)
Bernie White	SNAKE SELEJKO (1983)
Nancy Wickwire	PHYLLIS ANDERSON (1972–73)
Mary Charlotte Wilcox	JANENE WHITNEY (1969)
Steve Wilder	JACK DEVERAUX (1997–98)

Donna Wilkes	PAMELA PRENTISS (1982–83)
Brett Williams	TODD CHANDLER (1980)
Jeff Williams	DAVID BANNING (1970–73)
Sheila Wills	LEXIE BROOKS (1988)
Cheryl-Ann Wilson	MEGAN HATHAWAY (1984–85)
Jane Windsor	EMMA DONOVAN (1985–87)
Ray Wise	HAL RUMMLEY (1982–83)
Karin Wolfe	MARY ANDERSON (1972–75)
Charlayne Woodard	DESIREE MCCALL (1991–92)
Robert S. Woods	PAUL STEWART (1986–87)
Katherine Woodville	MARIE HORTON MERRITT (1977)
Morgan Woodward	PHILLIP COLVILLE (1987)
Dan Woren	SHELDON (1987–90)
Wendell Wright	LLOYD PRESTON (1985)
Kai Wulff	PETROV (1983–84, 1986, 1991)
H. M. Wynant	ORBY JENSEN (1982–84)
Claire Yarlett	DR. WHITNEY BAKER (1990–91)
Amy Yasbeck	OLIVIA REED (1986–87)
Merritt Yohnka	JOEY (1984–90)
Francine York	LORRAINE FARR TEMPLE (1978)
Paul Zachary	SHAWN-DOUGLAS BRADY (1990)
John A. Zee	NICKERSON (1984–85)
Suzanne Zenor	MARGO ANDERMAN HORTON (1977–80)
Arianne Zucker	NICOLE (1998–present)
Mark Zuelke	JASPER (1998)

APPENDIX B
Fan Clubs

For The Show

Official *Days of Our Lives* Fan Club
P.O. Box 11508
Burbank, CA 91510–1508

NBC Daydream Team
(A club covering all the NBC soaps)
P.O. Box 2759
Toluca Lake, CA 91610–0759

DEAFinitely *Days*
(A club designed for hearing-impaired fans)
2921 International Drive
Suite 2005B
Ypsilanti, MI 48197–8552

For Current Castmembers

The Kristian Alfonso Fan Club
The Krista Allen Fan Club c/o Tommy L. Garrett Jr.
The Jaime Lyn Bauer Fan Club
The Drake Hogestyn Fan Club

The Lauren Koslow Fan Club
The Peggy McCay Fan Club
The Austin Peck Fan Club
The James Reynolds Fan Club
The Louise Sorel Fan Club
The Alison Sweeney Fan Club (code 0919)
—ALL CAN BE REACHED—
c/o *Days of Our Lives*
NBC-TV
3000 W. Alameda Avenue
Burbank, CA 91523

The Official Jensen Ackles Fan Club
(run by his family)
P.O. Box 850812
Richardson, TX 75085-0812

Deidre Hall Fan Club
(run by Hall herself)
P.O. Box 6026-109
Sherman Oaks, CA 91413

The Joseph Mascolo Fan Club
(run by Mascolo himself)
11684 Ventura Blvd.
Suite 5026
Studio City, CA 91604

For Former Castmembers

The Lakeside Association
(supporting Mary Beth Evans and Stephen Nichols)
37663 Charter Oaks Boulevard
Clinton Township, MI 48036

The Stephen Nichols News Network
NNN East Coast
P.O. Box 466966
Mt. Clemens, MI 48046
—OR—
The Stephen Nichols News Network
NNN West Coast
8806 Ogden Street
Ventura, CA, 93004

Wally's Friends
(supporting Wally Kurth)
P.O. Box 640
Merrick, NY 11566-0640

Crystal's Club
(supporting Crystal Chappell)
c/o Christine Tobias
35627 Conovan Lane
Fremont, CA 94563

J. Eddie Peck
c/o Peggy Goldsmith
221 S. Illinois Street
Streater, IL 61364
Steven Wilder
c/o Lynn Orsanti
7103 Winchester Avenue
Ventnor, NJ 08046-1926

The Official West Coast Pat Delaney Fan Club
633 East 4th Street
Berwick, PA 18603

Bibliography

Carey, Macdonald. *The Days of My Life*. New York: St. Martin's Press, 1991.

Harrington, C. Lee and Denise D. Bielby. *Soap Fans: Pursuing Pleasure and Making Meaning in Everyday Life*. Philadelphia: Temple University Press, 1995.

Hyatt, Wesley. *The Encyclopedia of Daytime Television*. New York: Billboard Books, 1997.

LaGuardia, Robert. *Soap World*. New York: Arbor House, 1983.

Lofman, Ron. *Celebrity Vocals*. Iola, Wisconsin: Krause Publications, 1994.

McNeil, Alex. *Total Television: A Comprehensive Guide to Programming from 1948 to the Present* (Fourth Edition). New York: Penguin, 1996.

O'Neil, Thomas. *The Emmys: Star Wars, Showdowns and the Supreme Test of TV's Best*. New York: Penguin, 1992.

Rout, Nancy E., Ellen Buckley, and Barney M. Rout (editors). *The Soap Opera Book: Who's Who in Daytime Drama*. West Nyack, New York: Todd Publications, 1992.

Russell, Maureen. *Days of Our Lives: A Complete History of the Long-Running Soap Opera*. Jefferson, North Carolina: McFarland, 1995.

Schemering, Christopher. *The Soap Opera Encyclopedia* (Second Edition). New York: Ballantine, 1987.

Waggett, Gerard J. *The Soap Opera Book of Lists*. New York: HarperCollins, 1996.

——. *The Soap Opera Encyclopedia*. New York: HarperCollins, 1997.

Zenka, Lorraine. *Days of Our Lives: The Complete Family Album*. New York: HarperCollins, 1995.

My research also relied on back issues of: *Soap Opera Weekly, Soap Opera Digest, Soap Opera Magazine, Soap Opera News, Soaps In Depth, Soap Opera Update,* and *TV Guide.*

ANSWERS TO QUIZZES

the Perils of Marlena
1. d; 2. a; 3. a; 4. d; 5. b; 6. b; 7. a; 8. b; 9. b; 10. b

the Original Supercouple
1. b; 2. d; 3. c; 4. c; 5. c; 6. a; 7. b; 8. b; 9. d; 10. c

AKA
1. a; 2. a; 3. b; 4. d; 5. a; 6. c; 7. a; 8. b; 9. c; 10. d

the Rumors of His Death
1. TRUE; 2. FALSE; 3. FALSE; 4. TRUE; 5. FALSE;
6. TRUE; 7. TRUE; 8. FALSE; 9. FALSE; 10. TRUE

the Ultimate Days of Our Lives Quiz
the 1960s: 1. b; 2. c; 3. b; 4. d; 5. d

the 1970s: 6. b; 7. b; 8. b; 9. c; 10. c

the 1980s: 11. d; 12. b; 13. b; 14. c; 15. a

the 1990s: 16. b; 17. b; 18. b; 19. c; 20. b

21. ALICE HORTON, Addie Olson Williams, Julie Olson Williams, David Banning, SCOTT BANNING

22. Forrest Alamain, John Stevens, Roman Brady

23. Drake Hogestyn, Deidre Hall, Robert Kelker-Kelly, Peter Reckell

24. Tony DiMera (DEAD); Renée Dumonde (DEAD); Megan Hathaway (DEAD); Benjy DiMera (ALIVE); Lexie Carver (ALIVE); Elvis Banks (ALIVE)

25. Susan, Sister Mary Moira, Thomas, Penelope

Index

B

Barber, Andrea, 124, 169–70

Barnett, Eileen, 21

Barrows, Samantha, 170

Barry, Patricia, 33, 51

Battaglia, Matt, 47, 100, 146

Bauer, Jaime Lyn, 40–41, 88, 104–6, 110, 121, 207

Bays, Michael, 87, 112

Behar, Joseph, 154–55, 159

Bell, Bill, 15–16, 70, 153, 155, 161, 169

Benet, Brenda, 22–23, 61

Berger, Mike, 95

Biggs, Richard, 38, 97, 98, 99, 123, 174

Billingsley, Dickie, 169

Billy Vera and the Beaters, 139

Bissett, Josie, 127

Boyd, Tanya, 40, 89, 106, 131

Brainard, Michael, 96

Bregman, Tracey E., 85–86, 167

Brennan, Melissa, 112, 120

Bromka, Stella, 54

Brooks, Jason, 71, 74, 90, 176

Brown, Peter, 92, 99, 122–23

Browne, Kale, 45

Burgi, Richard, 103

Burton, Steve, 96

Buzzi, Ruth, 139

C

Caccialanza, Lorenzo, 100, 105, 115, 134

Caine, Adam, 42, 89, 147

Cameron, Stephanie, 42

Campanella, Joseph, 160

Carey, Macdonald, 14, 28, 32–33, 54, 78, 87, 93, 95, 154
awards, 152–55, 161, 167, 169–70

Chapman, Judith, 48, 98

Chappell, Crystal, 39, 54, 60, 63, 91, 98, 103, 106, 111–12, 174, 209

Chase, Allan, 13

Chase, Ariana, 86

Cheatham, Maree, 28, 64, 90, 95, 102, 143

Chiles, Lois, 47

Clark, Christie, 49, 51–52, 58, 92, 104, 165, 178

Clarke, John, 26, 89, 123, 156

Clarke, Mindy, 123

Clary, Robert, 16, 21, 88, 130

Clooney, Rosemary, 143

About the Author

GERARD J. WAGGETT is a leading expert on soap operas. He is the author of *The Soap Opera Encyclopedia, The Soap Opera Book of Lists, The Official General Hospital Trivia Book, The As the World Turns Quiz Book, The Official All My Children Trivia Book,* and *The Soap Opera Puzzle Book.* He has written about soap operas for *Soap Opera Weekly, Soap Opera Update,* and *TV Guide.* He is a graduate of Harvard College and holds a master's degree in English from the University of Massachusetts.

also available from
RENAISSANCE BOOKS

Party of Five: The Unofficial Companion
BY BRENDA SCOTT ROYCE
ISBN: 1-58063-000-6 • $14.95

Hercules & Xena: The Unofficial Companion
BY JAMES VAN HISE
ISBN: 1-58063-001-4 • $15.95

Law and Order: The Unofficial Companion
BY KEVIN COURRIER AND SUSAN GREEN
ISBN: 1-58063-022-7 • $16.95

Homicide: Life on the Street: The Unofficial Companion
BY DAVID P. KALAT
ISBN: 1-58063-021-9 • $16.95

The Girl's Got Bite: An Unofficial Guide to Buffy's World
BY KATHLEEN TRACY
ISBN: 1-58063-035-9 • $14.95

Hogan's Heroes: Behind the Scenes at Stalag 13
BY BRENDA SCOTT ROYCE
ISBN: 1-58063-031-6 • $14.95

NEW FOR 1999

Soap Stars to Superstars: Celebrities Who Started Out in Daytime Drama
BY ANNETTE D'AGOSTINO
ISBN: 1-58063-075-8 • $14.95

The Ultimate Another World Trivia Book
BY GERARD J. WAGGETT
ISBN: 1-58063-081-2 • $9.95

TO ORDER PLEASE CALL
1-800-452-5589